Confederate Courage on Other Fields

Confederate Courage on Other Fields

Four Lesser Known Accounts of the War Between the States

by MARK J. CRAWFORD

McFarland & Company, Inc., Publishers

Jefferson, North Carolina, and London

Library of Congress Cataloguing-in-Publication Data

Crawford, Mark J., 1954–
Confederate courage on other fields : four lesser known
accounts of the War Between the States / by Mark J. Crawford.
p.   cm.
Includes bibliographical references and index.
ISBN 0-7864-0720-4 (illustrated case binding : 50# alkaline paper) ∞
1. United States—History—Civil War, 1861–1865—Anecdotes.
2. Confederate States of America—History—Anecdotes.
3. Dinwiddie Court House, Battle of, Dinwiddie, Va., 1865.
4. Confederate States of America. Army. North Carolina Infantry Regiment, 23rd—Biography.
5. United States—History—Civil War, 1861–1865—Personal narratives, Confederate.
6. Missouri—History—Civil War, 1861–1865—Social aspects.
7. United States—History—Civil War, 1861–1865—Social aspects.
8. Violence—Missouri—History—19th century.
9. United States—History—Civil War, 1861–1865—Hospitals.
10. Military hospitals—North Carolina—Kittrell—History—19th century.
I. Title.

E484.C77   2000
973.7   99-50233

British Library Cataloguing-in-Publication data are available

Manufactured in the United States of America

*McFarland & Company, Inc., Publishers
Box 611, Jefferson, North Carolina 28640
www.mcfarlandpub.com*

In memory of my mother, Janet Patricia Crawford,
who nurtured my interest in the Civil War at an early age by reading me
"Old Glory at the Crossroads" from the *Chicago Tribune* comics,
telling me stories about her grandfather,
and driving for days to visit Civil War battlefields.
It is to her I owe my love of history and the written word,
and immeasurable gratitude.

Contents

I. THE SOUTH'S "SUNSET CHARGE": THE BATTLE OF DINWIDDIE COURTHOUSE, VIRGINIA, MARCH 31, 1865   3

A small force of Confederates marched for days through knee-deep Virginia mud to fight Sheridan's cavalry at Dinwiddie Courthouse on March 31, 1865. Despite fatigue and hunger, they launched a hard-hitting attack that drove the Federals back nearly a mile. The 1st and 5th North Carolina Cavalry Regiments lost over half their fighting force in a dramatic charge across a rain-swollen stream nearly 100 yards wide, where men were swept away and drowned.

II. "I'LL LIVE YET TO DANCE ON THAT FOOT!": THE CIVIL WAR EXPERIENCES OF COLONEL CHARLES C. BLACKNALL, 23RD NORTH CAROLINA INFANTRY   57

A wealthy plantation owner, Charles C. Blacknall left the comfort of his estate to fight for the Confederacy. Composed by a dynamic, well-educated man who loved the written word, his letters home reveal the hardships of an officer's life in the army, and his changing relationship with his family. After surviving Gettysburg and Johnson's Island, his refusal to let surgeons amputate his foot after the Third Battle of Winchester led to his death in November 1864.

III. An Eye for an Eye:
An Episode from Missouri's Civil War   89

The pro-Confederate southeastern counties of Missouri were some of the most war-torn in the state. Severe measures by Union authorities, including the seizure or destruction of property owned by Southern sympathizers, led to widespread hatred for Federal soldiers. The swirling violence, including a civilian massacre and retaliatory executions, became so great that President Abraham Lincoln interceded to request that nothing be done "merely for revenge." The destruction of homes and fields left hundreds of families on the verge of starvation by the end of the war.

IV. Rebel Resort of the Dead:
The History of General Hospital Number One,
Kittrell's Springs, North Carolina   135

This former exclusive hotel and resort was converted into a field hospital by the Confederate government in 1864–1865. The suffering of its soldiers is told largely through the stories of the chief surgeon and the hospital chaplain, who recorded personal observations and the last words of several of the soldiers who died there. Many of the victims included teenaged "boy-soldiers" from the North Carolina Reserves who perished from typhoid fever and pneumonia, adversaries their youthful courage could not overcome.

Acknowledgments

The South's "Sunset Charge": The Battle of Dinwiddie Courthouse, Virginia, March 31, 1865

Bryce A. Suderow, a Civil War historian and researcher in Washington, D.C., graciously shared his many materials on the Battle of Dinwiddie Courthouse, and his knowledge of the cavalry operations during the Appomattox campaign. He also furnished a detailed analysis of the Federal casualties from the battle.

The Photograph Department at the North Carolina Division of Archives and History kindly supplied the photographs of a number of North Carolina cavalry officers. This photograph department is by far the most efficient, accommodating, and pleasant one I have ever dealt with. Their very reasonable costs underscore their commitment to making their materials available to historians and the public; I also appreciated their trust in not insisting on prepayment.

Dan Robbins of Richmond, Virginia, the owner of the Adams house, shared with me its rich history, including stories of its supposed hauntings.

"I'll Live Yet to Dance on That Foot!": The Civil War Experiences of Colonel Charles C. Blacknall, 23rd North Carolina Infantry

Ben Ritter, an archivist in Winchester, Virginia, was very generous with his time in helping search for materials pertaining to Charles C. Blacknall. His efforts helped locate "Waverly," the house in which Blacknall convalesced, and the story of Waverly's ghost.

Ken and Tricia Stiles, the owners of Waverly, graciously gave me a tour of their home, and allowed me to spend the night.

Two others who are as interested in Charles Blacknall as I am are John Bass of Spring Hope, North Carolina, and Milton Woodard of Pikeville, North Carolina. Bass kindly shared the many materials he had gathered on the Blacknall family, as did Woodard, Blacknall's great grandson. Their generosity is much appreciated, as is their commitment to recording the life of this valorous Confederate officer.

An Eye for an Eye: An Episode from Missouri's Civil War

This story would not have been possible without the interest and generous assistance of many people. I would particularly like to thank Jerry Ponder of Mason, Texas, for all his help, the valuable information he supplied, and his photographic skills. His generosity with his time and his source material has made this piece of history much more complete.

John L. Margreiter of St. Louis, Missouri, furnished valuable source material, reviewed the manuscript, conducted research, and kindly took a number of photographs. Patsy Creech of Troy, Missouri, provided information on James and John Wilson and their photographs. Sidney and D. D. Brown supplied additional information on James Wilson. Doris Riewald of Thousand Oaks, California, supplied the image of James Madison Kitchen. Shirley G. Ladd of Cape Girardeau, Missouri, and Laverne Papworth of Troy, Michigan,

furnished many details about Asa Ladd and his family. Mrs. Edward E. Lawson of Bowling Green, Missouri, provided information on Simon Branstetter and his family. Jack Mayes and Marvin L. Dinger of Ironton, Missouri, were very helpful in researching Franz Dinger. My sister, Ann Crawford, was most generous with her time and kindly typed and proofed the manuscript.

I would also like to thank the following individuals and organizations: Nancy Sandleback and Eliza Uhlig, manuscript specialists at the Western Historical Manuscripts Collections, Ellis Library, University of Missouri-Columbia; reference specialists Susan Yeshilada and Laurel Boeckman, State Historical Society of Missouri, Columbia, Missouri; Martha Clevenger, Archivist, and Jill Sherman, Pictorial History Collection, Missouri Historical Society, St. Louis, Missouri; Jack G. Grothe and Charles Staats II (Jefferson Barracks Cemetery photographs), Sons of Union Veterans of the Civil War William T. Sherman Billy Yank Camp 65, St. Louis, Missouri; William E. Lind, Military Reference Branch, Textual Reference Division, National Archives, Washington, D.C.; Mrs. Marian Barnett, Norfolk, Nebraska (photograph of Phillip McKim); D. L. Atchison, Director, Jefferson Barracks National Cemetery, St. Louis, Missouri; John Pellarin, U.S. National Park Service, St. Louis, Missouri; John N. Ferguson and R. P. Baker, Arkansas Historical Commission, Little Rock, Arkansas; Frank Bigger, Pocahontas, Arkansas; Eugene W. Braschler, Fairdealing, Missouri; Doniphan Public Library, Doniphan, Missouri; Mrs.

Mary Collins, Poplar Bluff, Missouri; Robert Monroe, Hawk Point, Missouri; Earl Greeson, Neelyville, Missouri; Mr. and Mrs. Robert Epps, Brandon, Florida; Terry Schwarz, Raleigh, North Carolina; Reverend Charles F. Rehkoph, Archives of the Diocese of Missouri, St. Louis, Missouri; Ira Crawford, Neelyville, Missouri; O. Bryan England, Historian, Department of the Army, Rock Island, Illinois; John White, reference specialist, Southern Historical Collection, University of North Carolina, Chapel Hill, North Carolina; Andrew Ponder, Hardy, Arkansas; Mrs. Coralee Paul, researcher, St. Louis, Missouri; Colonel Harold B. Simpson, Hill College History Complex, Hillsboro, Texas; Robert Bearsford, Wellesville, Ohio; Bill Fannin, Missouri State Museum, Jefferson City, Missouri; Lynn Wild, Norfolk Public Library, Norfolk, Nebraska; James Kincade, Pocahontas, Arkansas; Lawrence Dalton, Randolph County, Arkansas; and Jeff Flannery, Manuscript Division, Library of Congress, Washington, D.C.

Rebel Resort of the Dead: The History of General Hospital Number One, Kittrell's Springs, North Carolina

On one of my many trips between Raleigh and Washington in 1986, when I had to slow to 45 mph passing through Kittrell, I decided to take a few minutes and visit a Confederate cemetery that I knew was nearby. After walking among the graves, I spoke with local residents about the town's Civil War history. I later located materials from St. James Church at the North Carolina Division of Archives and History.

Marshall W. Butt, Jr., of Portsmouth, Virginia, generously supplied information and photographs regarding Dr. Holt F. Butt, his great grandfather. His help and interest are much appreciated.

William E. Lind (now retired) of the Military Archives Division, National Archives, Washington, D.C., assisted me on my visits to the archives and helped me sort through the various medical files in the Confederate records.

Roger Jones and the very efficient Photograph Department at the North Carolina Archives in Raleigh supplied the photographs of the Reverend M. M. Marshall.

The staff at the Museum of the Confederacy in Richmond, Virginia, especially researchers Trudy L. Gay and Lynn Stanley, were very helpful in researching a number of the Confederates buried in the Kittrell Cemetery.

Finally, I would like to thank the following people for their help during my research: M. Q. Plumblee (deceased), Mrs. F. M. Lyon, Mary Louise Finch Lewis, Lawrence E. Wood, Terry Schwarz, Mrs. H. H. Cunningham, Norma F. Butt, Mrs. Guy M. Beaver, Walter Brodie Burwell, Doris B. Frye, Macy Kennedy, and Mary Gordon Elliot.

Rebecca DuBey of Stoughton, Wisconsin, kindly compiled the index.

Mark Crawford • Fall 1999

Preface

When most of us think about the Civil War, we think about big battles—Bull Run, Antietam, Shiloh, Gettysburg, the Wilderness—the gruesome collision of giant lines of men that shaped our national history. Yet thousands of men endured great hardships or were killed in smaller campaigns during the war. Their sacrifices are largely forgotten, merely footnoted, or part of a larger statistic. The important role of noncombatants is similarly dismissed; these people include physicians, ministers, and the civilian support of troops and guerrilla units. Civilian casualties often resulted because of their commitment to the Confederate cause. The accomplishments and sacrifices of both Confederate soldiers and civilians in lesser-known Civil War events are documented in this book, many for the first time.

Why the lesser-known? Because larger events are built from smaller ones, and a deeper understanding comes from knowing both. These forgotten pieces of history are important because the sacrifice of a Confederate soldier who died in a skirmish, or on a scouting patrol, or from disease, is as great as one who died in Pickett's Charge. These stories are also important because they explore different theaters of conflict on various levels, and contribute to a better understanding of the Civil War and the human spirit.

Exhaustive research from 1984 to 1996 uncovered a variety of information from private, local, state, and national sources that document these pieces of Confederate history. Many of the photographs in this book have never been published before. It is hoped the reader will find the variety of new Confederate material informative, thought-provoking, and poignant.

The South's "Sunset Charge" details the Battle of Dinwiddie Courthouse,

Virginia. Fought nine days before the end of the war, it is considered by some to be the last Confederate victory. Besides showing the still-intact willingness of the Confederate army to attack against great odds, the battle demonstrates the superiority of Union weapons: Union cavalry armed with 7-shot and 15-shot repeating rifles held back a much larger Rebel force armed with muzzleloaders during the day-long fight.

There are few well-written, descriptive accounts of the war by Confederate soldiers that also reveal emotional and personal change. **"I'll Live Yet to Dance on That Foot!"** is taken largely from the Civil War letters and diaries of Colonel Charles C. Blacknall of the 23rd North Carolina Volunteers. Wounded at Gettysburg and later at Winchester, the seemingly indestructible Blacknall died in 1864 after refusing to let surgeons amputate his foot. Because he is such an honest man in his letters and openly expresses his feelings, the reader can witness the man change as he becomes consumed by the war.

Intense sectionalism and hatred are profiled in **An Eye for an Eye**. As the title implies, retaliatory violence, often directed at uninvolved soldiers and citizens, escalated in southeastern Missouri during the Civil War. Harsh Union policies alienated pro–Confederate citizens, who then supported guerrilla activities more vigorously. With definite parallels to the 1968 My Lai Massacre in Vietnam, 60 civilians, many of them women and children, were killed by Union troops on Christmas Day in 1863. The Union struggle to deal with guerrillas and "irregular" troops in southern Missouri is not much different from present-day efforts to suppress international terrorism.

Rebel Resort of the Dead is the history of General Hospital Number One, a Confederate field hospital that operated in Kittrell's Springs, North Carolina, in 1864–1865. It explores the terrible effects of disease, which soldiers often feared more than the battlefield. The original hospital log book, and handwritten observations by the hospital chaplain (including, occasionally, a soldier's last words), were discovered during the research. Because many of the patients were "boy-soldiers" who perished from disease, the role of the North Carolina Junior Reserves, a little-known unit, is also profiled.

I

The South's "Sunset Charge": The Battle of Dinwiddie Courthouse, Virginia, March 31, 1865

Introduction

Histories of the 1865 Appomattox Campaign in Virginia mention the Battle of Dinwiddie Courthouse only briefly, choosing instead to focus on larger events. This fight is typically regarded as the opening action to the Battle of Five Forks, which occurred the following day.

The opposing forces at Dinwiddie Courthouse were small, on the order of about 10,000 men each, and the outcome did not change the course of the last nine days of the war. Yet the sacrifice was great for certain regiments on both sides, which fought valiantly to achieve success in what one seasoned Confederate veteran said "was the most fearful and fiercest battle we were ever in."[1] It is for these men that this story is being told.

The spring of 1865 found the Confederate States of America in a perilous position. Vastly outnumbered by the Union Army, General Robert E. Lee's Army of Virginia manned the long arc of earthworks and trenches that protected the cities of Richmond and Petersburg, Virginia. The Union army, commanded by General Ulysses S. Grant, was over twice the size of Lee's, and had spent a comfortable winter behind its works, which bristled with redoubts, cannon, and abatis. In some

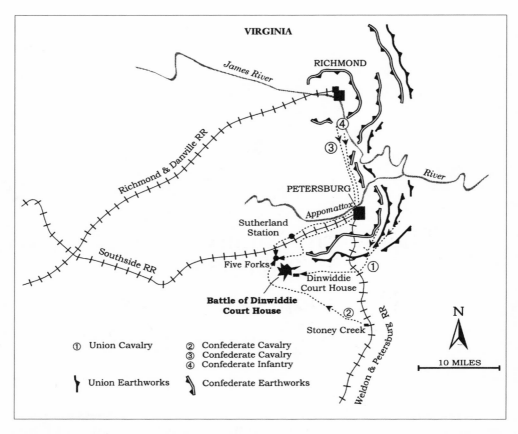

VIRGINIA

RICHMOND

James River

Richmond & Danville RR

PETERSBURG

Appomattox River

Sutherland Station

Southside RR

Five Forks

Dinwiddie Court House

Battle of Dinwiddie Court House

Stoney Creek

Weldon & Petersburg RR

① Union Cavalry

② Confederate Cavalry
③ Confederate Cavalry
④ Confederate Infantry

Union Earthworks

Confederate Earthworks

N

10 MILES

Distribution and movement of Confederate and Union troops prior to the Battle of Dinwiddie Courthouse (author's collection).

places the lines were as few as 100 yards apart, and the opposing pickets regularly conversed and visited. The Union soldiers were confident, sensing that Grant would soon strike the deciding blow that would end the dreadful war. Southern morale was not as high, because of winter hardships, increasing rates of desertion, and the knowledge that they would have to fight such a large, well-supplied, and persistent enemy (Grant had not turned back since he had taken command of the Union army in 1864).

The Confederates in the trenches were also helpless to stop the relentless northward movement of General William T. Sherman's Union forces through Georgia—the dreadful "march to the sea."

Lee realized that this threat was the gravest yet for the Confederacy. In addition to protecting the capital city, his defenses shielded the only remaining line of supply and communication: the Southside Railroad. And should Richmond fall, the Southside Railroad would be his line of retreat westward to General Joseph Johnston's army of 20,000 men in North Carolina and another stand against the aggressive Union army.*

As the ground thawed, and the rains and mud came, the Union camps began to stir, and Lee knew a Union offensive was imminent. It was possible that Grant would try to breach his line, but the Confederate defenses were strong and well-designed, and would be costly to take.† It was more likely that Grant would try to turn his right flank, or join Sherman's army coming up from the south, either of which would cut off Lee's line of retreat by seizing the Southside Railroad. Lee's only choices would be to strike immediately and hope for success, or let the cities fall into Union hands, and withdraw his army before Grant could attack. But if the Union army turned his right flank and took the railroad, his army was doomed.

General Sherman and his army won important battles at Averasboro (March 16) and Bentonville (March 19) in North Carolina, and were within 120 miles of the Petersburg defenses. Lee, desperate to disrupt the Union plans, launched a night attack on Fort Stedman on March 25. The Confederates failed to support their initial breakthrough of the Union line, and the attack ultimately failed. Lee suffered over 4,000 casualties on that day. Afterwards he wrote to Jefferson Davis that the only option remaining was to withdraw from Richmond and Petersburg, and unite with Johnston in North Carolina. Thus

it was imperative that Lee keep the enemy off his right flank until his preparations for leaving Petersburg were complete, and the roads had dried out enough for the weakened horses to haul the hundreds of wagons.

During this time General Grant had met with his corps commanders to discuss the spring offensive. Grant was worried that Lee might escape and reinforce Johnston. If this happened, it would prolong the war, be viewed by the country as a defeat, and further demoralize the war-weary public (many of whom were critical of President Lincoln's administration and favored a treaty to end the bloodshed). A resounding victory was therefore critical to the Union cause. Indeed, as Robert E. Lee had feared, Grant gave orders that would move two infantry corps out of the entrenchments to attack Lee's right flank. General Phil Sheridan and his cavalry were to strike out for Dinwiddie Courthouse in advance of the infantry. Dinwiddie Courthouse lay beyond the extreme right of the Confederate line, and Sheridan's task was to lure the Confederates away from their breastworks into open battle. If they chose not to fight, Sheridan was to go on a raid and strike the Southside Railroad, or join Sherman. At the very least Lee would have to move men to deal with this threat, further weakening his defensive perimeter. If that happened Grant might be able to score a crippling breakthrough elsewhere along the line.

The Southside Railroad led westward to the operating rail lines of the Richmond & Danville and Piedmont Railroads, which were also principal lines of supply, communication, and transport.

†*Grant ordered a frontal assault on Lee's works at Cold Harbor on June 3, 1864, where the Union army lost nearly 7,000 men in less than 30 minutes. As in many other battles during the war, support was mismanaged and other attacks uncoordinated, resulting in a horrible number of casualties—yet the attack came close to succeeding.*

Lee had to act immediately. After consulting with General James Longstreet, he ordered nearly all the available cavalry, and the only force of infantry he could spare, to the crossroads of Five Forks, about four miles beyond the Confederate right, and a few miles north of Dinwiddie Courthouse. The road that led directly to the Confederate rear and the railroad went through Five Forks. The sleepy little hamlet was suddenly the focal point of the spring campaign, and absolutely critical to the Confederate cause. The race to Five Forks had begun.

Confederate Preparation

The Confederate cavalry was below strength, since a number of men who had been sent to the interior to winter their horses had not returned. The cavalry force, totaling about 4,000 men, consisted of the divisions of Generals William H. Lee, Fitzhugh Lee, and Thomas Rosser. Orders were received on March 28, and the cavalry camps were suddenly busy rounding up men at the remount camps and hospitals, gathering supply wagons and ambulances, and drawing mounts, rations, and forage.* "Fitz" Lee was ordered to Petersburg to receive instructions personally from his uncle, General R. E. Lee. Upon his ar-

rival the next day the commander-in-chief informed him that Union troops were heading for the Southside Railroad, and that he was giving him full command of the entire cavalry corps. His mission: get to Five Forks as quickly as possible, join ranks with the infantry, and drive Sheridan back.

The infantry chosen for this important task was commanded by General George E. Pickett. Three of his brigades (commanded by Generals Corse, Terry, and Steuart) were to join with two brigades detached from General Anderson's corps, which was manning the extreme right of Lee's line. These regiments were also depleted, and Pickett's force totaled about 6,000 men. Pickett's orders were to march to Five Forks and unite with Fitz Lee's cavalry. Pickett was given overall command of the combined infantry-cavalry force (10,000 men), that was envisioned by Lee and Longstreet as a mobile unit that would strike wherever necessary to protect the Confederate right.

Union Preparation

Sheridan was dismayed by the possibility of being detached from the main army to wreck railroads, or to go south to join Sherman. He wanted his hard-

*Captain Frederick Colston, of the Ordnance Board, recollected that "the state of the armament of the cavalry was giving much trouble to the Ordnance Department, owing to the variety of arms carried by the men. It was actually the case ... that a single company might have half a dozen different kinds of carbines.... It was almost impossible to supply the different kinds of ammunition at all times and consequently many men would be out of action when most needed. General Lee had directed that an effort be made to correct this state of affairs, and I was to go down to the cavalry division ... have the men paraded and, by swapping the arms, try to make squadrons at least uniformly armed. This would be a difficult and disagreeable task, as these arms had been captured by men in battle in most cases and were, consequently, valued and their exchange would be objected to.... I started out on [the 29th] ... [and] was afraid to ride my own fine little mare down amongst the cavalry and I took an old white horse which was used in the train.... [Colston never carried out Lee's order]."[2]

fighting cavalry to be in "at the death" of the Confederacy. Grant noticed that Sheridan was disappointed after reading his instructions, which prompted him to take Sheridan aside and tell him

> that as a matter of fact, I intended to close the war right here, with this movement, and that he should go no farther. His face at once brightened up, and slapping his hand on his leg he said "I am glad to hear it, and we can do it."[3]

The cavalry received General Grant's orders on the 28th, and each man drew a horse, five days' rations, 40 rounds of ammunition, and 30 pounds of forage. Sheridan's three divisions (commanded by Generals George Crook, George Armstrong Custer, and Thomas Devin) totaled about 9,500 men, armed with repeating rifles.* Knowing his superior's expectations for a rapid and hard-hitting expedition, and the poor conditions of the muddy roads, Sheridan brought a minimum of wagons and only eight artillery pieces. After quick preparations†, the cavalry broke camp very early in the morning on March 29 and moved out for Dinwiddie Courthouse to find the right flank of the Confederate army.

March 29, 1865

The Confederate Cavalry

It was a beautiful dawn, and the day was "clear, calm, and pleasant."[6] Fitz Lee's men had been on the extreme left of Lee's defenses the previous day, and had marched via Petersburg so that their commander could receive verbal instructions from Robert E. Lee. After leaving Petersburg, Fitz Lee's division camped at Sutherland Station, ten miles south of Petersburg on the Southside Railroad (Fitz Lee conferred briefly with General Pickett, who passed through with his troops later that night). The weather had turned drizzly and cold in the late afternoon, and soon a hard and miserable rain set in.

The divisions of Rosser and William ("Rooney") Lee had joined forces at Stoney Creek Station, where they had been sent to forage their horses. The horses were in poor condition and "jaded" (exhausted). The cavalrymen had hoped for a few days to rest their mounts, and as usual were uncertain about orders, plans, and where the next few days would take them; one guessed that "a big battle is inevitable in this section—soon, if Grant attempts a movement on the Southside RR." They left in the early afternoon after

---

*Sheridan's troopers were armed with the 7-shot Spencer rifle and the 15-shot Henry rifle. The Confederates called this weapon "that damned Yankee rifle that can be loaded on Sunday and fired all week." A regiment of Union cavalry armed with the repeating rifle had twice the firepower of a Confederate regiment fighting with muzzle-loaders.[4]

†Preparations were not quick enough for the liking of the 6th Ohio Cavalry. A. D. Rockwell remembered that before leaving camp "for some time we stood in a long line, and soon attracted the fire of a spiteful little battery or two in plain sight. At first these shells fell short.... A third shot ... buried itself in the hip of [a] horse. Still another of these conical six pounders ... went under the shoulder blades and completely through the body of a soldier ... [who] died a few minutes later. Orders now came to change our position, and none too soon.... It has always seemed to me that the affair was stupidly unnecessary."[5]

receiving their marching orders. After marching ten miles they camped at dark on the Boydton Plank Road battlefield, still scarred from last year's fighting and littered with debris and the occasional set of human bones.* Although the weather had been sunny and clear the past few days, the roads were soft and muddy, and the progress slow with mud up to the saddle girth. With few tents, the men spent an uncomfortable night in the steady, cold rain.

The Confederate Infantry

Pickett gathered his scattered brigades and sent them south on the Southside Railroad to Sutherland Station. His orders were to report to General Anderson on the extreme right of Lee's lines at daylight the next morning (the 30th). The departure of his troops was impossible to conceal from the Union lookout stations. There was no room on the crowded rail cars for the unfortunate 1st and 7th Virginia regiments of Terry's brigade, which were forced to march the distance to Sutherland Station. The first of Pickett's men arrived about 9:00 P.M., moved out a few miles, and slept in the cold rain until the rest of the infantry arrived. They were then roused about 2 A.M. to continue the march. The night was very dark and chilly, and the rain was relentless. When they arrived about 8:00 in the morning, soaked and caked in heavy mud, they were formed in line of battle on Anderson's right flank.

The Union Cavalry

The lead elements of Sheridan's division left before dawn. Saving the better roads for the infantry, the cavalrymen moved cross-country through woods and fields, following roads where they could find them. They passed somberly through Ream's Station battlefield, still littered with wreckage and debris. One soldier remembered that

> there had been repeated fighting and all the region round about was seamed with the scars of it. Massive lines of earthworks stood out like veins on the face of the country.... [T]hrough the empty window-frames of the few buildings there, the wind whistled plaintively.[7]

Another wrote that "this place is unpleasant, for it reminds us all of how our present expedition may be nothing more than the old story of flanks extended, attacked, defended, and intrenched."[8]

They arrived at Rowanty Creek to find the bridge had been burned. A band of Rooney Lee's cavalry was visible on the opposite bank. The water was muddy and high, and a few men from the 1st Maine Cavalry, lumbermen and rail-splitters who "could knock up a bridge while the horses were being watered," swam across and felled two large trees across the floodwaters. The enterprising Yankees lashed the trees together and fashioned a covering of rails and hay. "It was a rickety structure," remembered an officer of the 13th Ohio Cavalry, "but we crossed safely in columns of four."[9] A skirmish ensued that resulted in the

---

*The Battle of Boydton Plank Road on October 27, 1864, was the result of General Grant's attempt to cut the Southside Railroad. His advance was driven back by a Confederate infantry-cavalry force after bitter fighting. Many of the men trying to sleep on the wet ground or huddled around fires were veterans of that battle.

capture of some Confederate prisoners, who revealed that their cavalry was moving on a parallel course.

Sheridan's advance arrived at Dinwiddie Courthouse about sunset after a 25-mile march, and drove away a patrol of Confederate lookouts. (Sheridan's rear guard rode into town about sunrise the following morning.) Custer's division was escorting the wagon train, and was hopelessly bogged down in the Virginia mud. By nightfall the wagons had traveled a mere seven miles, and were camped at Rowanty Creek. Custer's weary soldiers worked all night in the cold rain, and gained another three miles by morning.

According to Sheridan, "Dinwiddie Courthouse ... was far from attractive in feature, being made up of half a dozen unsightly houses, a ramshackle tavern propped up on two sides with pine poles, and the weather-beaten building that gave official name to the cross-roads."[10] Sheridan and his staff took the tavern for their headquarters, and compelled the two young women who lived there to make coffee and play the piano while the officers sang songs. Sheridan's mood was further buoyed by a message from Grant that stated

Major General Fitzhugh Lee, commander of the Confederate cavalry during the Battle of Dinwiddie Courthouse (U.S. Military History Institute).

I now feel like ending the matter, if it is possible to do so, before going back. I do not want you, therefore, to cut loose and go after the enemy's roads at present. In the morning, push around the enemy, if you can, and get on to his right rear. The movements of the enemy's cavalry may, of course, modify your action. We will act all together, as one army, here, until it is seen what can be done with the enemy. The signal officer at Cobb's Hill reported, at 11:30 A.M., that a cavalry column had passed that point from Richmond toward Petersburg, taking forty minutes to pass [Fitz Lee].[11]

Overall, it had been a good day of movement for the Federal forces, and they had beaten the worst of the weather. Two of Sheridan's divisions (Generals Crook and Devin) had made it to Dinwiddie Courthouse as planned, and Custer would be up the following day with the trains. By occupying the courthouse, Sheridan forced the Confederate cavalry to make a wide sweep south and west to arrive at Five Forks. This added more exhausting miles and treacherous fords, making the march through deep mud and pelting rain that much worse for the Confederates. Both infantry corps had moved into position as planned, extending the Union left all the way to Sheridan at the courthouse.

Delighted with his new orders from Grant, Sheridan retired for a few hours of sleep in a feather bed upstairs.

March 30, 1865

The Confederate Cavalry

The weather was abominable. Rain fell hard all day, sometimes in wind-driven, blinding sheets. Fitz Lee's soaked troopers arose early from their uncomfortable sleep and marched directly to Five Forks, which they found unoccupied. Encouraged, Fitz Lee advanced a force down the road toward Dinwiddie Courthouse, anxious to locate Sheridan.

The divisions of Rooney Lee and Rosser also rose early and marched all day and night in the mud and rain. The trains were hopelessly behind and abandoned. The detour around Dinwiddie Courthouse delayed them considerably.

Streams were over their banks and the fords were difficult: horses swam, and the ammo chests were packed across by hand.[12] A soldier in the 35th Virginia Cavalry wrote that we "had to swim Stoney Creek too and expect we will have to swim it again tonight—I am sorry I am a soldier now."[13] The weakened horses sank to the saddle girths in mud with every step. The troops did swim Stoney Creek again in darkness, and at 3 A.M. halted on the White Oak Road and rested for a few hours, close to Five Forks.

The Confederate Infantry

Pickett's weary men stayed in the battle line until noon, thankful for the rest. The rain fell in sheets. Union divisions were visible maneuvering in their front. General Lee arrived about ten in the morning to confer with his field commanders. They rode along the lines, and Lee peered at the enemy through his field glasses. Lee "seemed to be in a bad humor," remembered Lieutenant Gordon McCabe.[14] "It was inferred by many of us that preparation for a great battle was in progress," wrote another.[15] Shortly afterwards Pickett was ordered to take his three brigades, the brigades of Ransom and Wallace (both at half-strength) from Anderson's command, six artillery pieces, and march directly west along the White Oak Road to reinforce Fitz Lee at Five Forks.

The Union Cavalry

The Union troopers were unimpressed by the countryside around

Dinwiddie Courthouse. "Seven acres out of every ten," wrote a news reporter, "are covered by a small young growth of almost impenetrable pines, so commonly seen in this country on worn out lands."[16] A soldier observed the country was "low and flat, covered with forest and thick underbrush, and abounding in swamps and sluggish streams that drained the water slowly."[17] Indeed, the woods and fields resembled a swamp when it grew light enough to see. One wrote that

> the rain, that faithful and untiring ally of the Confederacy ... came down as though the supply were inexhaustible.... The familiar red clay, which kneads up into a thick and pasty mass, and forms great ridges as the horses in sets of fours follow in each other's footstep had given place to a black and yielding sandy loam, which in the flooded fields, became almost a quicksand in which horse and rider were in danger of sinking out of sight.[18]

It had been a rough night—those that had been able to sleep did so under rubber ponchos. Many men had simply stood around fires all night, trying to stay warm.

Crook's Second Division drew good duty—most of the men remained in camp by the fires while the others picketed the roads and stream crossings leading to Dinwiddie Courthouse from the west.

The First Division, commanded by General Devin, had arrived just an hour before, barely having time for coffee, when it was ordered out in the morning to find the enemy. Devin used nearly all his men as he advanced strong reconnaissance patrols north on the Dinwid-die Courthouse Road toward Five Forks. Devin was centered on the road, with regiments dispersed (and entangled) in the briary woods on the right and left flanks. The 6th Pennsylvania Cavalry, the center regiment, found the thick pines to be "dismal and gloomy." Shortly after leaving camp, and wading rain-swollen Gravelly Run, they came upon a small brigade of Confederates "lying quietly in the woods."[19] These soldiers were the vedettes from Fitz Lee's cavalry.

Sheridan

Grant was worried about the weather, and the incessant rain. His theater of operations was turning into a quagmire, and his men were moving at a mud-caked crawl. Concerned that well-timed movements of troops would be impossible, he telegraphed Sheridan to temporarily suspend his cavalry operations.

Sheridan was irritated. After receiving the order, he mounted his horse and rode away to find Grant. It was a slow, wet ride to Grant's headquarters. Sheridan passed countless "field wagons hopelessly embedded in the glutinous soil, drivers and mules had given it up."[20] Lieutenant Colonel Horace Porter of Grant's staff saw Sheridan arrive, not at a "pacing gait ... [but] at every step driving [his horse's] legs knee-deep into the quicksand with the regularity of a pile-driver." Another observer wrote that "water dripp[ed] from every angle of his face and clothes." With a cheerful voice and feverish eyes Sheridan told a group of Grant's staff officers that he was "ready to strike out tomorrow and go to smashing things"—Porter remembered he was "pacing up and down, [and that] he chafed like a hound in the leash."[21] Later he had a 20-minute private consultation with Grant, who conceded with a simple "we will go on."[22] Sheridan rode away enthusiastically, and on his way back stopped and consulted with General G. K. Warren, the commander of the infantry on his immediate right. When he arrived he was dismayed to find Warren asleep in the middle of the afternoon.

Custer and the Wagons

The men having the hardest time of things on March 30, Union or Confederate, were in Custer's Third Division. They had to deal with the wagon trains. Foot by foot, mile by agonizing mile, the mud-soaked troopers pushed the wagons forward. They had worked 24 hours the previous day, and this day was no different, except that the rain was harder. (An engineer with the infantry indicated that this "was the worst day for moving trains [I ever] had in all [my] experience. A train of 600 wagons, even with the aid of 1000 engineer troops, was fifty-six hours in going five miles.")[23]

Custer's men were using logs to corduroy the road, a thankless and infuriatingly slow task: "Nothing short of corduroying every inch would enable the train to move, and then it must be very slowly and carefully, or legs of mules will be broken," wrote a soldier.[24] The troopers had to unload wagons and physically lift them to move them forward. John Hannaford of the 2nd Ohio Cavalry wrote that

first a force was cutting down the pine trees that grew near by, these flung into the road were laid as near together as the[y] would lie, then other[s] were covering these with fence rails, & still another force were dragging the tops of the pine trees & covering the rails with pine limbs, even all this was disappear-[ing] a foot or two under the water & mud when the wagons were on it, the bottom seemed literally to have tumbled out.[25]

The water was so deep in some of the roads that the logs floated, and "were an obstacle instead of a benefit."[26] Hannaford also recalled the plight of a fellow soldier whose horse plunged into a water-filled hole in the road. The soldier, loaded down with weapons, ammunition, and a full haversack "came off in the middle of it & came blame near drowning, disappearing entirely in the mud & water."[27]

Working all day and night, the train advanced another ten miles, and was still five miles from Dinwiddie Courthouse.

A Cavalry Skirmish: Fitz Lee vs. Devin

Cautious skirmish fire erupted between the 6th Pennsylvania Cavalry and Fitz Lee's vedettes in the dark woods along the Courthouse Road. The 2nd Massachusetts Cavalry and 1st U.S. Cavalry were called up to reinforce the 6th Pennsylvania, and this impromptu brigade began to push the Confederate skirmishers back on their reserves. A member of the U.S. Cavalry recalled that "this affair ... was a scramble through the mud and brush, against an enemy always concealed, who yielded without much resistance after delivering fire, the pistol being the principal weapon used on both sides."[28] Confederate resistance stiffened, and the Union men began to fall back in retreat. The 7th Michigan Cavalry was brought up in columns of squadrons with sabers drawn, and charged the Confederates. With shouts of "Sheridan!" they broke the Confederate line, the enemy fleeing "the field in a confused rout, leaving in our hands ... a large number of prisoners."[29] They followed the retreating Confederates to Five Forks, where they "took refuge behind some ... rifle-pits, which were seen to be bristling with the muskets of a strong force posted there."[30]

Captain Henry Kuhles of the 2nd Massachusetts Cavalry (U.S. Army Military History Institute).

Shortly afterwards "the [balance] of the brigade was brought forward & we advanced & attacked their works but found them to strong & to well defended for us & we returned to the skirmish line." Captain Kuhles of the 2nd Massachusetts Cavalry "without a follower ... galloped his horse definitely up to and over the breastworks.... I think that his daring must have struck such amazement into the enemy that they re-

frained from shooting him at such close range."[31]

Devin's men fell back a short distance and desultory skirmishing occurred throughout the day. In the afternoon the 6th New York Cavalry operating on the left was surprised by a Confederate force in the thick and confusing woods, and was forced to fall back.

The reconnaissance had served its purpose: Fitz Lee and Sheridan had found each other, and Sheridan now knew that Fitz Lee was fortifying his position with breastworks, and was prepared to hold it.

The Confederate Infantry

Pickett's men moved out along the White Oak Road, west towards Five Forks, about one o'clock in the afternoon. General Matt Ransom, who commanded the two brigades from Anderson's corps, remembered that "some of the heaviest showers of rain I think I ever saw" fell that afternoon.[32] Colonel Gordon McCabe, who rode with Colonel "Willie" Pegram and the artillery force, wrote that

> our flank being exposed to the enemy, they harassed us with small bodies of cavalry without intermission. Gen'l Pickett, instead of pushing on, stopped, formed a regiment in line-of-battle, and awaited some attack. Much valuable time was lost this way. A line of skirmishers marching on our flank would have been ample protection.[33]

The Union troopers who were attacking Pickett's column and wagon trains were the regiments that Devin had deployed to his right in the morning. General Steuart's brigade was the rear guard on the march and skirmished with the pesky cavalry all the way to Five Forks. The rain was relentless. The mud was deep and caked to the men, horses, and wagons, and they were being fired at constantly by the Yankee horsemen. An infantryman recalled that

> during the firing, some ladies and children were noticed by our men in

a field some hundred yards or more in our front, running about in great alarm, not knowing where to seek refuge from the balls whizzing through the air.... General Corse ... sent a courier to tell them to plunge into the woods to their right and come into our lines.[34]

The infantry arrived at Five Forks about sunset, and immediately began building breastworks. The weariest regiments, the 1st and 7th Virginia, who had marched more than any of the other commands in the division, were put out to drive away the Union cavalry. They pushed them down the Dinwiddie Courthouse Road, and then remained out on picket duty all night about a mile in front of Five Forks. The rest of the infantry, without blankets or food, lay down and tried to sleep in the rain. For many it was too wet and cold to sleep, and privates and officers alike stood beside fires all night long.

Like Grant and Sheridan, Robert E. Lee's first goal had been accomplished: Pickett and Fitz Lee were holding Five Forks. It was now time to strike Sheridan a blow like he had never felt before.

The Union Cavalry

Devin's men fell back to their campsite from the previous night, and "when the miserable evening fell, we very uncomfortably went into camp to find rations all soaked, and blankets all wet, and spongy beds under leaking shelters. Those who had the heart to whistle, whistled 'Home, sweet Home,' and the rest of us lay still under the trickling canvas, hungry, cold, and tired."[35]

Sheridan and his staff had another festive evening at his headquarters as the storm raged outside. All was going well so far. Officers "betook [them]selves to merry song, and harmony ruled the hour."[36]

Pickett and Fitz Lee

Pickett was still not at full strength. He anxiously awaited the arrival of Rooney Lee's and Rosser's cavalry divisions, still struggling to reach Five Forks in the rainy darkness somewhere to the west.

Pickett, Fitz Lee, and the other commanders held a "council of war" from 3:30 to 6:30 A.M.—smoking, telling stories, and working out a strategy for the attack that would start in the next few hours.[37] There is no record that Rooney Lee or Rosser was present at this meeting. Lee was close to Five Forks, when at three in the morning his troops halted for rest on the White Oak Road. It is possible that he rode forward and met with Pickett and Fitz Lee. Rosser indicated that he did not see Pickett and Fitz Lee until eight o'clock the following morning. A cavalryman from Lee's division remembered that they first came upon their own infantry, on the move, the following morning, Pickett's attack already in motion. Thus it is uncertain whether Lee was there, at least in part, for the strategy session. If he did not attend, it is possible that Pickett had no idea if the rest of his cavalry was going to arrive in time.

March 31, 1865

It had been a cold and wet night, but when dawn came the rain had stopped, and the skies cleared by ten in the morning. The sun was out. Despite having little rest, spirits of the men on both sides were high—the rain was done, the marching was done, and there was a battle to be fought. George Pickett had been a forgotten man since the Battle of Gettysburg in 1863, and today was his opportunity to save the Confederate Army. No doubt Fitz Lee was excited by his first role as supreme cavalry commander, and wanted to perform well and score an important victory for his uncle, Robert E. Lee. Every soldier sensed the importance of this day, and despite the hardships and fading hopes of independence, they were still proud Confederates and anxious to fight Sheridan.

The Union troopers were also ready for a fight. They had complete faith in Sheridan, and knew that they had infantry on their right. Devin's men had scouted the Confederate position at Five Forks, and knew the ground in their front. Custer's men, after 48 hours in the mud with wagons and mules, were especially longing for the front. Custer, in particular, was always loath to miss a fight.

Pickett

By most accounts the infantry was on the move by nine o'clock in the morning, having been preceded by Rosser's and Lee's cavalry divisions.

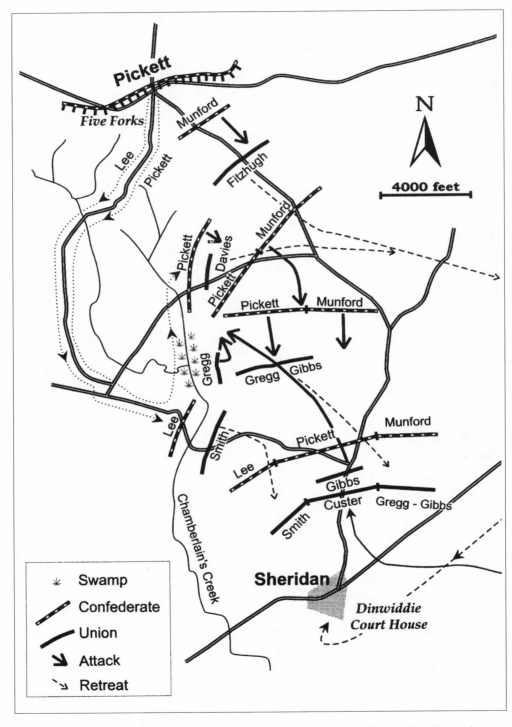

Troop movements during the Battle of Dinwiddie Courthouse (author's collection).

Chamberlain's Run at the Fitzgerald Ford crossing, at the present day (photograph by the author).

Pickett's plan was to leave Fitz Lee's division (now commanded by General Thomas T. Munford) to hold Five Forks and the road to Dinwiddie Courthouse, where they had found Devin's men the day before. Using a local guide, Pickett would then swing south along the west bank of a stream known as Chamberlain's Run, and launch a surprise strike on the Union left flank. Fitz Lee wrote in his official report that

we attacked the very large force of the enemy's cavalry in our front at Five Forks…. Munford, in command of my old division, held our lines in front of the enemy's position, whilst the remaining two divisions of cavalry, preceding the infantry, moved by a concealed wooded road to turn and attack their flank. A short stream, strongly defended at its crossing, presented an unexpected

obstacle to the sudden attack contemplated.[38]

Chamberlain's Run was normally a typically narrow, sluggish Virginia stream, but after two days of rain it had turned into a raging torrent, nearly 100 yards wide, and up to neck-deep in the channel. It was clogged with debris and floating timber, and the sides of the creek were thick with submerged briars and underbrush. The first Confederates to arrive were Lee's cavalry, who gazed at the roiling muddy water with concern.

Crook

Crook commanded the Second Division and guarded the roads that

The position on the road just west of Fitzgerald Ford where the first Confederate cavalrymen deployed (photograph by the author).

crossed Chamberlain's Run and led to Sheridan's left flank. General Charles Smith's brigade (1st Maine, 2nd New York Mounted Rifles, 6th Ohio, and 13th Ohio Cavalry) guarded Fitzgerald Ford. About a mile to the north, Chamberlain's Run was crossed by another road at Danse's Ford: this position was picketed by General Eugene Davies's brigade (1st New Jersey, 10th New York, 24th New York, and 1st Pennsylvania Cavalry). Crook's last brigade, commanded by General Gregg, held the ground between Smith and Davies on the east side of Chamberlain's Run.

On the previous day squadrons from the 1st Maine Cavalry and 2nd New York Mounted Rifles had watched Fitzgerald Ford. They had kept themselves busy constructing breastworks of logs, rails, and "anything that would stop a bullet."[39] This morning elements of the 1st Maine and 2nd New York were positioned behind their defenses, watching for the enemy in the dark, wet woods across the creek.

Crook was anxious to know what was in his front. A battalion from the 1st Maine was ordered to scout beyond the stream. They swam their horses across and immediately ran into Rooney Lee's cavalry, which had just arrived. Sharp skirmishing began. The 1st Maine advanced a short distance, driving back the Confederate pickets. A few minutes later they saw the gray shapes of mounted and dismounted Confederate cavalry hurrying into line, and heard officers shouting orders. The Union soldiers prudently withdrew under heavy

General Charles Smith's Union troopers straddled the road at this position just east of Fitzgerald Ford (photograph by the author).

fire, and "on arriving at the creek the men threw themselves into the water among the horses, which protected them somewhat from the Rebel fire, and on gaining the other shore were rallied and fell back slowly."[40]

Rooney Lee

That "Rebel fire" came from General Rufus Barringer's North Carolina brigade, a part of Rooney Lee's cavalry division. About eleven o'clock in the morning, Barringer's force, led by the 1st and 5th North Carolina Cavalry, "soon drove the [enemy] in panic and rout, forcing him across the stream, over waist-deep, all in the wildest haste and confusion."[41]

Barringer deployed the dismounted 1st North Carolina regiment in the woods north of the ford, forming a line about 150 yards long. The 5th North Carolina regiment, also dismounted, formed in line at the water's edge south of the ford. The 2nd North Carolina was ordered to follow the 5th. Beale's brigade of Virginia cavalry was held in reserve. Colonel William H. Cheek, commander of the 1st North Carolina, stated that

> the stream was very much swollen by recent heavy rains, and at places was impassable by reason of briars and swamp undergrowth. In my immediate front it was over one hundred yards wide and as deep as the men's waists.[42]

A private from the 5th North Carolina recalled that the water was

Brevet Bigadier General Charles H. Smith, whose brigade held the crossing at Fitzgerald Ford during most of the battle (Tobie, *History of the First Maine Cavalry*).

it we went," wrote veteran Fred Foard. "It was a nasty position, but we did it." The soldiers moved into the cold, fast water and immediately faced a "galling" fire from the repeating rifles on the other side of Chamberlain's Run.[45] Daniel B. Coltrane remembered that bullets peppered the water, and "men were shot down in the ford, swept off by the current and actually drowned."[46] In places the water was as deep as their armpits, and the men had to carry their weapons and cartridge boxes above their heads as they advanced.

much deeper with us than where the [First] was, even if it was the ford. So deep ... and [with] other obstructions of fallen timber on both sides of the stream, that it could not be crossed, for battle, except at the ford. It would swim a horse twenty feet below the ford.[43]

Barringer's plan was to advance the 1st and 5th North Carolina across the creek, quickly followed by the dismounted 2nd North Carolina regiment, that was to "deploy fast in line of battle to the left and above the ford, completing and connecting the line between Cheek and Colonel James H. McNeil [commander of the 5th North Carolina] and drive the enemy."[44]

"Every man was at his place and at

Soldiers were rapidly falling. When they reached the other side, Cheek's regiment took shelter in the heavy woods, which "afforded as much protection to one side as the other."[47] McNeil and his men, after passing through a "scrubby thicket" along the far bank, emerged into an open field.

Before the 2nd North Carolina moved forward to take the center, General Lee ordered a mounted charge by the 13th Virginia Cavalry of Beale's brigade. The men were shocked by the order: as one put it, "this was absolute murder." As the lead squadron plunged their mounts into the deep water at the ford, "the bullets patter[ed] in the water like hailstone."[48]

J. Armfield Franklin of Company F, 13th Virginia Cavalry, described the charge:

> The banks here on both sides [of the ford] are very steep, while the ford is so rough that it is impossible to cross in any order. Then, nothing is harder than to form cavalry under fire, when horses as well as men are more or less excited....
>
> Our squadron led the advance. The bushes were so thick on each side of the road, which came down obliquely from the ford, that fifteen steps from the creek, one was screened from observation from the opposite side. To avoid drawing the fire of the enemy as much as possible until they could go in, the second squadron halted here until we should get out of the way....
>
> We reached the opposite bank.... Spurring up into line in a little clearing on the right side of the road, we gave a lively cheer, and dashed up the hill, our horses sinking above the fetlocks at every step.[49]

Crook

The firing alerted Smith to the new development in his front. The rest of the 1st Maine, stationed along the road about a mile to the rear, and behind a slight rise, was ordered at a "quick step" to the front. The men ran past "wounded soldiers and officers on their way to the rear mixed in with the led horses."[50] The 2nd New York Mounted Rifles held the woods against Colonel Cheek and the 5th North Carolina, the fighting Indian-style and nearly hand-to-hand. The 1st Maine battalion, badly outnumbered and falling back in the open field, continued to deliver a hot repeater fire into the exposed ranks of McNeil's regiment. As the rest of the 1st Maine appeared on the field

> less than a hundred yards away ... in the road, just coming out of the thicket [that edged the creek], is a body of the enemy's cavalry, charging toward the regiment, swinging their sabres and yelling like demons.... That column of charging cavalry was a sight worth living to see. On they came, brave fellows, turning into the field a short distance from the creek, and still charging onward ... but the repeaters ... were too much for them. On they came, but came no nearer. Men and horses went down, and the head of the column remained in nearly the same place.[51]

Barringer

The squadron from the 13th Virginia Cavalry faced a concentrated, murderous fire from the 1st Maine cavalry advancing toward them on foot. "Then was the time," wrote Franklin, "for the [rest of] the squadrons to have dashed across to our support." The second squadron was

> afraid to come around the turn into the storm of bullets that now swept the ford, and the others could not pass them, though their curses were loud and deep when they knew from the fierceness of the firing that [we were] being "used-up".... Lt. Moiler cried "Goddamn them they won't help us boys! In retreat—March!" We found the [ford] choked up with horses, all rushing to the rear as fast as spurs and oaths could propel the writhing mass of men and horses.... Thus were men and horses sacrificed in vain, through the cowardice of our comrades, and the stupidity or culpable ignorance of our general.[52]

Colonel William H. Cheek, commander of the 1st North Carolina Cavalry (North Carolina Division of Archives and History).

[We] rushed at them on the enemy's side of the stream and tried to rally them, and especially to keep them off the [2nd]. But they were panic-stricken; not even appeals to "look at those North Carolinians crossing here" could halt those horsemen, breaking the line of the [2nd] and pushing them down in the deep water at the lower side of the ford. The enemy was so exultant over their sight of the fleeing squadron that they advanced and redoubled their already furious fire on McNeil and the ford, where the column of the [2nd] was now helplessly cut in twain by that mingled mass of mounted men, while McNeil's ammunition was almost exhausted.[53]

The collapse of the mounted cavalry charge was disastrous for the Confederates. McNeil had been waiting for the 2nd North Carolina "to form on my left that we may charge and carry those works." He sent a courier to Barringer to "hasten the [2nd] over." Two companies of the 2nd had started to cross behind the mounted cavalry. A soldier recalled that as the squadron fled

Just as the 1st Maine's moment was won, Barringer's moment was lost. Some of the 5th North Carolina men, armed with muzzle-loaders, were down to only two cartridges. Enfilading fire was beginning to come from the woods as the Union troops curled around the 5th's right flank. Colonel McNeil was killed by a bullet through the head at short range in the thickest of the fighting. As some of his men struggled to bring his body back across the creek, "the entire line gave way" before the murderous fire. This compelled the 1st North Carolina to recross the creek as well. Private John Miller Monie of the 1st North Carolina cavalry wrote that

> during this fearful encounter I received a severe wound in my leg.... After falling I found that I was in more real danger than in the line of battle, as I was in range of the fire of our own men as much as from that of the Federals. I lay on the field for some time, the bullets falling thick and fast all around me. Many men were lying in the field wounded and dying, our Captain among them.... In no battle, and I was in most of them, have I ever seen men killed and wounded as I saw here.[54]

Colonel James H. McNeil, commander of the 5th North Carolina, who was killed after leading his men in the first crossing of Chamberlain's Run at Fitzgerald Ford (North Carolina Division of Archives and History).

The short fight, which lasted about 30 minutes, was over. A survivor remembered simply that "somebody had made a grave mistake."[55]

Munford and Devin

Devin moved cautiously north along the Dinwiddie Courthouse Road, about nine in the morning. The pace was slow, due to the mud and stiff skir-

mishing from enemy videttes and pickets.

General Munford was ordered by Fitz Lee to hold the road to Five Forks, and to attack the enemy in his front as "soon as [he] heard the rattle of [Fitz Lee's] guns, in sufficient volume to indicate a serious engagement, and then to join my command to his." As Fitz Lee rode off, he waved his hand and shouted to Munford in his wry way that "we'll meet again in the paradise of the faithful, or somewhere else more handy and convenient."[56] Munford kept his men in the woods, and left the division's horses behind them at Five Forks.

Pickett

The infantry arrived at Fitzgerald's Ford about 11 o'clock in the morning after a two-hour march. Despite the fatigue, "everybody was in fine spirits." They heard the fighting off to their left, and the "sharp, peculiar ring of the cavalry carbine."[57] Officers' bodies, draped over horses, were being brought off the field, and the dead and wounded were being hauled from the fast current of Chamberlain's Run.

Pickett decided that the infantry could not cross at Fitzgerald's Ford,* and the soldiers were "hurried up" a mile to the north. "They moved slowly up the run, looked in upon Irvine Gregg, whose fine brigade, protected by a marsh, could laugh at them, and passing by him, found both a better piece of country for their designs, and prospect of success, in front of General Davies," wrote a Union officer.[58] Using a local guide, Pickett's force had arrived at Danse's Ford, expecting to find a bridge. "But on reaching the spot," remembered an infantryman, "[we] found that the bridge had been washed away." The infantry, with Terry's brigade in the lead, soon discovered the crossing was guarded by more Federal cavalry: Davies's brigade.

Davies

Davies's men were spread out in the woods on either side of the Danse Road, a mile to the north of Smith at Fitzgerald Ford. They too had crossed the creek early in the morning, and captured a few Confederate pickets, who indicated that Pickett's infantry was approaching. In preparation the men extended and strengthened their line of rail breastworks, and waited for the enemy.

Pickett

Pickett ordered General Terry to take the ford. This crossing was almost as treacherous as Fitzgerald's Ford a mile below. Terry advanced the 24th Virginia Regiment, followed by the 11th Virginia, under heavy repeater fire from the Federal breastworks. "The firing soon became sharp and vigorous," wrote Major Robbins of the 1st New Jersey Cavalry. "We had great advantage in position, being behind works and on much lower ground than they enemy, who were without covering and at easy range. Many of the enemy fell before our withering fire."[59]

As the 24th Virginia attacked the ford, Rosser and his cavalry division appeared (Pickett had ordered him to go with Rooney Lee, and then, if possible, to break away and raid Sheridan's trains near the crossroads of Hargrave's). When the 11th Virginia started to cross, the enemy "evacuated the ford and hid

---

The reason Pickett cited for not crossing at Fitzgerald's Ford does not make sense, since two cavalry regiments (and an enemy battalion) had previously waded across the stream and occupied the opposite shore. An attack of infantry and cavalry at this point would have overwhelmed Smith's brigade.

himself on the eminence just beyond." Generals Rosser and Dearing were down with Pickett, giving orders. "General Rosser appeared on the scene, on horseback, and was urging the men about," wrote a regimental commander. "I did not know him and wanted to know what he had to do with my command."[60] More regiments crossed the creek and began to move in on the flanks of Davies's brigade.

Davies

Davies's men fought well at first, the 1st New Jersey being the hardest hit. Flanked to the left and right, they resisted until the enemy was 15 yards away and fell back to higher ground along the road behind them. The 10th New York Cavalry came up to support the 1st New Jersey, delivered two or three volleys, and then "went rapidly to the rear, leaving my battalion to cover their shameful retreat," wrote Major Robbins of the 1st New Jersey.[61]

Pickett

Pickett's infantry began to pour across the ford—Terry on the left, Corse on the right, and Steuart coming up from behind. The men took time to form, and faced more stubborn resistance from the new Union position up the road. Federal artillery appeared and began shelling the Confederate position. A cannonball killed General Terry's horse, which fell on Terry, breaking his leg and forcing him to leave the field. By this time the Confederate cavalry had

fallen in to the left of the infantry, and they moved steadily forward. The Federal position began to crumble and panic. The "led horses" were a few hundred yards behind in the dense pine woods, four horses held by a single trooper. The racket of battle was getting closer, and bullets were flying so fast that even the horses kept their heads down. Lines of communication were broken in the thick woods, which was full of horses, soldiers, bands, and separated regiments in confused retreat. General Davies was in the rear trying to direct the fall-back.

Munford

Munford had been waiting anxiously to hear the sounds of battle. As Pickett's infantry began to advance and collapse Davies back on top of Devin, Munford advanced on Devin's men through the dense pine woods. Devin had received an urgent request for reinforcements from the 1st New Jersey, and knew Davies was being routed on his left. A Union soldier remembered that "we were deployed in the woods ... five paces apart. The woods were alive with Johnnies, and we were all mixed up in hand-to-hand encounters."[62]

Gregg and Gibbs

Gregg's brigade (the 4th, 8th, 16th, and 21st Pennsylvania Cavalry Regiments), posted on the east bank of Chamberlain's Run between Smith's Brigade at Fitzgerald Ford to the south and Davies's brigade at Danse's Ford to the north, stood "to horse" all morning, ready to support either Smith or Davies. They had exchanged desultory shots with the Confederate infantry who had passed on the other side of the creek that morning, looking for a place to cross. "Several bands of the corps were posted at different points," remembered a Pennsylvania trooper, "playing lively music, and much enthusiasm prevailed among the men, who believed that important movements were about to take place."[63] The men knew from the sounds of the fighting to the north that Davies was being driven back.

General Gibbs and his regiment, in reserve, listened to the din of battle around them. An aide from Sheridan rode up with orders to attack the Confederate infantry that was pushing Davies and Devin. Gregg's brigade left its position along Chamberlain's Run to reinforce Gibbs.

The cavalry quickly advanced cross-country about a mile, dismounted, and ran north toward the sound of the fighting. A Pennsylvanian recalled that "the tramp of the enemy's troops through the undergrowth could be plainly heard, and [soon] we could see that the woods were grey with them.... They saw us too, just then, and halted to look to this new and unexpected enemy."[64]

The Federals launched a hard, surprise attack on the Confederate right. The Confederates had halted to re-form and wait for the rest of the division to come up, having driven Davies back to the crest of a hill. The 32nd Virginia was exposed on the extreme right, and was hit first in flank and rear. It was forced back in savage, hand-to-hand fighting,

exposing the 17th Virginia to surprise volleys that cut down soldiers. Nearly 40 Confederates were killed, wounded, or taken prisoner during the short encounter. A number were clubbed from behind. Gibbs wrote that his men hit the flank and rear of the passing Confederate flank and the "straggling riffraff in the rear of Pickett's division of infantry. Not much persuasion was required to induce these noncombatant wearers of the gray to throw down their muskets."[65]

Gibbs soon had a real fight on his hands, as the surprised regiments re-formed, and the 30th Virginia came up. The fighting was "close up and hotly engaged" as General Steuart's advance brigade instinctively turned toward the sound of the fighting.[66] "Our sudden and spirited attack threw them into some confusion, from which they soon recovered and attacked," wrote Pennsylvania trooper Andrew J. Lee.[67]

The Union troopers fell back to their horses, rode a short distance, and dismounted again to fight on foot. They charged again and drove back advancing Confederate skirmishers, and then fell back to a third defensive position. A steady and destructive fire had nearly exhausted their ammunition, and the dead and wounded were looted for cartridges. Gibbs definitely had Pickett's attention.

Pickett

Pickett had envisioned one unified, sweeping line driving the Union forces like sheep. Rosser's cavalrymen were to ride around the battle and raid the Federal rear, but that plan was abandoned when they fell in to assist Munford and Pickett in the early-afternoon fighting on the Davies-Devin front. Pickett finally had Munford and his infantry moving together, with Munford's right connected to Corse's left, and Terry on Corse's right. Steuart, Ransom, and Wallace were following behind for support. Fitz Lee, meanwhile, was still trying to get Rooney Lee's cavalry to force the crossing at Chamberlain's Run again.

Gibbs's attack had stopped the Rebel pursuit on Davies and Devin, and had bent the Confederate right back about 150 yards. This allowed Devin's panicky men to gather their wits and make it out of the woods to the Boydton Plank Road, and ride south to Dinwiddie Courthouse (they arrived at dark after the battle had ended). Stung by Gibbs's unexpected attack, and uncertain about the size of this force, Pickett ordered a right wheel and swung his east-facing battle line around to face south, and advanced on the new enemy. Colonel Stagg, commander of the Devin's 1st brigade, remembered that "all the force of the enemy seemed to move off to the left and go off through the woods."[68]

Sheridan

Sheridan was in trouble. His forces were scattered. His right, Devin's division, was falling back in confusion. The center, Gregg and Gibbs, was fighting a much larger infantry force that was pushing them steadily backward. The left, General Smith's brigade, had taken losses in a hard morning fight and still held the ford on Chamberlain's Run. Sheridan then called up Custer, and hoped that he had time to construct a defensive line that his men could fall back to in front of Dinwiddie Courthouse.

Lee and Barringer

The loss from the morning fight had been appalling. Barringer indicated that "in this short conflict ... twenty officers [were] killed and over one hundred men killed and wounded."[69]

During the afternoon the Confederates were hidden behind rocks and trees, exchanging random shots with the enemy. Because the enemy could not be seen through the thick woods and brush along the creek, four soldiers volunteered to be lookouts, and took positions behind pine trees to watch for Federal movements at the ford. "The enemy could see us distinctly whenever we would look from behind our trees, and the peculiar hiss of minies was incessant, all of our four trees being struck frequently," wrote one of the men.[70] It remained this way for two or three hours, and seven or eight soldiers were wounded by random firing.

About the same time that Pickett's infantry moved across Danse's Ford and attacked Davies, Pickett ordered Fitz Lee to join the advance and take Fitzgerald's Ford, the scene of the morning's bloody fighting. This was about two o'clock in the afternoon, and both Rooney Lee and Rufus Barringer were reluctant to do it. Fitz Lee threatened them with arrest if they did not carry out his orders. Soldiers with axes cut paths through the thick woods to the water. Barringer delayed the procedure for nearly two hours, until Fitz Lee arrived to oversee the attack in person. The Federals, who had spent the afternoon fortifying their lines, reported they could hear the Confederates busily chopping. Fred Foard, an officer on Barringer's staff was shocked that "the bloody work must all be done over again."[71]

Barringer asked for the order to be withdrawn, citing his severe loss earlier in the day. Fitz Lee refused. Barringer then requested that one of Rooney Lee's other brigades lead the assault. Rooney Lee would not substitute any of his men, stating that his brigades were under-strength.* He told Barringer to deploy his men as he saw fit and push the attack, and then rode away.

Smith

The Union troopers lay behind their breastworks and listened to the Confederates chopping trees and clearing their way to the stream. A soldier of the 13th Ohio Cavalry recalled that

> some of the Johnnies yelled over and asked who we were. Somebody said: "You will find out soon enough, if you come over here." Some of the boys said: "Johnny you had better look out; for Sherman is coming up behind you."

Johnny replied "Johnston will take care of him."[72]

Deadly sharpshooting continued across the water. The open field at the ford was especially murderous. The Ohio troopers in the woods by the ford needed ammunition, and volunteers were called for to ride across the field to the rear and retrieve it. George Fisher of Company M, 6th Ohio Cavalry, dashed through the bullets to return with a box of cartridges across his saddle—both box and trooper dived into the woods from the galloping animal. Other volunteers followed his example, and ammunition was passed along the line. An officer from the 1st Maine remembered that

> the regimental band came down in rear of the line, and before the boys knew it was there, struck up "Yankee Doodle," making those woods ring as they probably never did before. The boys received it with hearty cheers, and the rebels with yells and shouts of derision. In a short time a rebel band, over across struck up "Dixie," at which the boys in blue yelled. That being finished, the First Maine band played "Red White and Blue," and the rebel band responded with "Bonnie Blue Flag." And till late in the afternoon the two bands kept up a musical duel. Cheap talk was going on between the lines. As one of the Maine boys fired into the woods a rebel sent back a laugh of defiance, with the words "You'uns better keep your ammunition; you'uns may want it before night." Parts of the line called a truce on random firing, and began to quiz each other back and forth across the Run.[73]

---

*Fred Foard, one of Barringer's officers, wrote that it was actually Beale's Virginia brigade that was in front that day, and that Rooney Lee, in order to protect his Virginians from the severe loss he knew would occur, put the North Carolinians forward.

General Rufus Barringer, commander of the North Carolina Cavalry brigade at Fitzgerald Ford (North Carolina Division of Archives and History).

Lieutenant Jefferson L. Coburn of the 1st Maine Cavalry, as he appeared in 1894 (*Maine Bugle*).

Lee

General Barringer wrote that "the Run was still very full, covering the bottoms for seventy-five yards on either side of the channel, with only one crossing for mounted troops, and the banks everywhere obstructed by logs, brush, and other impediments."[74] Taking his time, Barringer decided to put the 1st North Carolina Cavalry in line,

dismounted, on the left of the road, in the same position they had started from in the morning, to "attack and draw the fire of the enemy." The 2nd North Carolina Cavalry would then carry out a mounted charge across the ford in column. The 5th North Carolina would remain dismounted with "bridle in hand, until the critical moment should arrive, to determine the part it should take."[75]

Beale's Virginia brigade was positioned by Rooney Lee on Barringer's left, to come to the support of either wing.

Pickett-Munford-Gibbs-Gregg

After Pickett turned south to face the new threat of Gibbs and Gregg, the scattered elements of Devin's Division fell back through the thick pine woods for a few miles by orders of General Sheridan. Relieved to find their led horses, they took a circuitous route back to Dinwiddie Courthouse via the Boydton Plank Road, and arrived at dark.

Pickett's line moved steadily southward, the right guiding on Chamberlain's Run. The terrain was hilly and densely wooded, with nearly impenetrable old pine fields, ravines, and gullies choked with briars and undergrowth. The soldiers struggled to stay in formation. The Union troopers made short, spirited stands and charges, and delivered an annoyingly constant repeater fire. At one point the 8th Pennsylvania was ordered to charge across an open field to attack a part of Pickett's command, facing "a murderous fire, losing very heavily, but, after a fight at very close quarters, driving the enemy from the woods. We were soon attacked by overwhelming numbers ... and forced to fall back." Again the dead and wounded were looted for cartridges. The Union men then formed to face two lines of Rebel infantry "moving in magnificent style, with long steady strides. When they neared us General Irwin Gregg, with the brigade flag in hand, rode along our line and ordered it to charge, and the brigade dashed forward with a cheer, breaking and driving the first line, but receiving a withering fire of musketry from the second line."[76]

The Confederates facing these hot pockets of carbine fire were Terry's and Corse's brigades. The brigades of Steuart, Ransom, and Wallace were following in reserve. Captain Henry A. Chambers of the 49th North Carolina Infantry of Wallace's brigade, described the noncombative role the reserve brigades had that day:

[W]e crossed [Danse's Ford] and formed a line of battle, and moved down the stream a mile or more. We passed through old pine field thickets and deep ravines. Occasionally we halted and listened to the contest going on below, the din of musketry, artillery and the savage yells of the struggling men. Now moving forward, now at a halt, now through the thickets of pine and now over ravines bordered by briers and brambles.... When it got dark we halted for the night.[77]

Custer

For a final defensive stand, Sheridan had chosen a slight rise of ground northwest of Dinwiddie Courthouse to which his scattered brigades could fall back and entrench. He wrote that "it was now about 4 o'clock in the afternoon and we were in a critical situation." His force had been cut in half, and Devin and Davies were out of the fight. Sheridan was anxious to see Custer.

Custer's Third Division had been listening to the fight all day as they wearily corduroyed the roads. Three or four miles away with the wagon trains, Custer was elated to receive Sheridan's urgent message from the front. He took Capehart's and Pennington's brigades and advanced toward the fighting at a gallop. It was about a two-hour ride in the mud to the front. Isaac Gause of the 2nd Ohio Cavalry recalled that

the front line was lonesome without Custer.... We made the best time possible, leaving the train to fall to any fate that might overtake it. On the route we passed hundreds of dead and wounded that lay in the mud or sat braced up by trees.... Some had arms in slings, and with their clothes cut open to bind up their wounds, and their faces and hands besmeared with blood and powder smoke, they made a pitiful looking sight.[78]

As they approached the front and heard the firing, Custer shouted

Captain A. W. Fenton, 13th Ohio Cavalry (Ohio Historical Society).

there was work ahead," wrote a Union trooper.

Fitzgerald Ford: The Sunset Charge

Barringer had been ordered at two o'clock to take the ford, and now it was past four o'clock and the sun was going down. As the men moved toward the water Captain A. W. Fenton from the 13th Ohio Cavalry remembered "we heard some Confederate officer give the command 'Forward! Guide right!' ... a Rebel yelled out 'wind up them guns, Yanks!' In a few minutes we heard their lines advancing."[81]

Barringer wrote that "when Colonel Cheek gave the command 'Forward!' the 1st moved off with a pride of step and confidence of purpose worthy of its best days. With line unbroken, it bore the whole fire of the enemy from all his works and all along the opposite shore."[82] Led by Colonel Cheek, the 1st North Carolina Cavalry moved boldly into the deep water, guns and ammo held high, as bullets swept the water around them. "As to drawing the fire of the enemy, this part of the plan was a great success," wrote Cheek. "A shower of lead met us as soon as we entered the water and was poured on us continuously until we

gleefully that "General Sheridan and those fellows up there don't know whether school is going to keep or not!"[79] His men quickly dismounted and formed the defensive line on Sheridan's rise, at first facing west toward Smith and Fitzgerald Ford. As Custer's band played "Garry Owen," the men busily constructed "the most miserable apology for breastworks [that] ever was seen, consisting of rotten fence rails [and] brushwood, with a little earth."[80] The sound of battle grew louder, and Custer's men could hear the cheers of the Confederates and see the blue forms of Gibbs's men falling back. "We knew that reached the fence on the other side." Nearly the entire brim of Cheek's hat was shot off during the crossing.[83]

When Cheek's men were halfway across, the 2nd North Carolina Cavalry charged across the ford, with the 5th North Carolina on its right. The First continued to cross as if on dress parade to "an old fence [that] ran between the creek and the first field, the water in some places extending through it and out into the open land. [We] halted at the fence, each man protecting himself as best he could."[84]

They continued to take a fierce fire as they waited for the 2nd and 5th to come up. Colonel Cheek and Lieutenant Colonel Cowles, "stand-

Union trooper Isaac Gause, 2nd Ohio Cavalry, postwar (author's collection).

ing in water up to our waists, were consulting what to do, when he was shot in the head and [almost] drowned."[85]

Beale's Virginians crossed on Cheek's left, and within "ten minutes the whole Yankee line was in flight."[86] The Confederates rushed over the works with cheer after cheer. The artillery had finally returned from Danse's ford, and taken position on a small hill. The gunners opened fire with short fuses. "In all my experience (and I had been in over sixty fights, great and small) I never saw a more splendid charge. They simply swept everything out of their way," wrote one of the artillerymen. Another soldier remembered that "the current was filled with the bodies of the dead and wounded; but on they still came, fording the stream with the water breast deep, and holding their muskets and ammunition above their heads, till they reached the shore."[87]

An Ohio cavalryman wrote that "the enemy advanced within 15 or 20 steps of us, while we mowed them down like grain before a reaper. Their line wavered, but their officers urged them

Major Paul Chadbourne of the 2nd New York Mounted Rifles, killed at Fitzgerald Ford (Tobie).

the advancing foe. The boys fought bravely—the enemy as bravely, keeping up a heavy fire and taking the fire of the Union troops without being checked in the least.... The enemy had a piece or two of artillery in position, and was throwing shot and shell into the woods, which rattled twigs, and sometimes large limbs, as well as their iron hail.... Above all the noise and confusion, the rattling of the carbines, the roar of the artillery, the screaming and bursting of shells, the commands of officers and the shouts of men, rose the shrieking, whining rebel charge-yell.[90]

Lee's men had finally taken the ford, and the Virginia regiments on their left had connected with infantrymen from Steuart's brigade. The sun was setting behind the trees, and long shadows crossed the field. The Ohio, New York, and Maine veterans fell back, but still fought with "dogged obstinacy.... The Federals would rally and re-form, only to be broken and dispersed," wrote a Confederate.

The stubborn retreat was anchored by the 1st Maine. A member of the 6th Ohio recalled that "this was the first time I had ever been in such a pell mell retreat. It was getting dark, everything was confusion and disorder."[91]

The Union withdrawal seemed to take forever. They came to a turn in the road, and behind them saw the welcome

on."[88] A member of Company B, 13th Ohio Cavalry, remembered that "our comrades were falling all around us; we lost more than half of our company in less than half an hour." "It was about as unhealthy in the rear as it was in the front," recalled another, "as a rebel battery had range of the road, and was playing havoc with our wounded."[89]

According to Lieutenant Colburn of the 1st Maine, when the charge commenced

the boys sprang to their places, and in an instant were pouring a heavy fire into sight of "a line of Union troops behind a breastwork of rails, but a short distance away."[92]

Custer

Most of Custer's men had settled in behind the crude breastworks. The 6th Ohio of Smith's brigade seemed to be in the greatest hurry to get back to the line, and had just arrived when Pennington's 2nd Ohio came up and moved forward about half a mile to slow down the Confederate infantry. Sheridan had shouted to Custer: "Do you understand? I want you to *give* it to them!"[93] The troopers rode north a short distance, dismounted, and ran to the shelter of a little knoll with a house on it (the Adams property). They passed through their retreating comrades from Gibbs's and Gregg's brigades. John Hannaford of the 2nd Ohio Cavalry wrote that

Captain B. F. Metcalf of the 13th Ohio Cavalry, killed during the second assault at Fitzgerald Ford (Ohio Historical Society).

> not a man of them stops ... and we turn from them with bitter words and dash on. We gain the knoll and house, and drive the skirmishers back. The Rebels keep coming and it was really magnificent to see them as they came, a double line, the men standing shoulder to shoulder ... as tho' on parade. The line halts and fires a unified volley at the house. From their open mouths I could see the rebel yell was echoing, but not a sound of it was heard, owing to the racket made by the balls on the weatherboards.[94]

"The face of the sun had now half descended behind the western hills, and the whole surface of the ground about it was bathed in one immense crimson bath," remembered a Union veteran. "Troops were constantly arriving on the ground where the Division colors were still seen flying."[95] The 2nd Ohio held the position for five minutes before

Looking west down the farm road that leads to the Adams house. The house was held for a short time by Custer's troopers before they were forced back by Pickett's infantry (photograph by the author).

retreating back to a fence line. The Confederates swirled around the Adam's house and fired at the retreating cavalry. "A storm of lead was flying, and the enemy charged and we broke. The ground we had come over was sloping and there was such a storm of lead I thought it best to follow up the swale," wrote Hannaford. Custer dashed up and down with the division flag but couldn't stop the retreat where "troopes were flying over the field like leaves in wild weather."[96]

One of Gibbs's men claimed that "our brigade had the worst of the fire, for we were nearer the jaws of death. It was the hottest fire I was ever in, and it was the harder for me to face, as I had no definite place to hold, and no specific instructions to fulfill. Wherever I stood it seemed as if I ought to be somewhere else. Many of our men fell."[97]

A member of the 2nd Massachusetts Cavalry (Gibb's brigade) was amazed that the advancing infantry "seemed to us utterly reckless of death. In the face of our severest fire they would swoop down upon us across an open field with such a careless swing, it seemed as if they enjoyed being on the skirmish line, and we suspected that they had such a miserable time of it in camp that they preferred standing up to be shot at."[98]

The Adams house as it looks today (photograph by the author).

As the last of the Maine men entered the works from Fitzgerald's Ford, a column of Confederate cavalry galloped up the road in hot pursuit toward the empty guns of Smith's brigade behind the rails. Capehart's men "opened so suddenly on their left flank as to cause it to recoil in astonishment, which permitted Smith to connect his brigade with Custer's."[99] The last remnants of Gregg's and Gibbs's brigades came back into the line a short time after Smith did.

Pickett's men continued to move toward the Union position. "Looking back," remembered a veteran, "the solid grey lines of the enemy's infantry could be seen advancing into the open ground, presenting such a tempting target that our eager artillerymen could not wait for their front to be cleared, but began pitching their shells over the heads of the retreating troopers."[100]

Pickett

Pickett's advance was cautious. "To our surprise, we were ordered to halt, although we could see the enemy still fleeing before us [Gibbs-Gregg]" wrote Colonel J. R. Hutter of the 11th Virginia

Infantry.[101] "We [lost] men at every step [of the advance]", remembered Colonel Arthur Herbert, commander of the 17th Virginia Infantry. "We are halted to dress upon the right brigade, who are not in the line of fire and can't see the enemy's panic. The halt is fatal. The enemy stand to their guns; again their skirmishers reform and cover their front."[102]

It had taken all day, but Pickett had gotten his men across Chamberlain's Run, outflanked the enemy, and split the Union forces. He had driven them back toward Dinwiddie Courthouse, and his men were connected in a long line of battle that was about half a mile from the poorly entrenched enemy. Sheridan was in a precarious position with only two of his three divisions together on his defensive line.

Sheridan

It was nearly dark. A mounted column arrived behind the 1st Maine's position, carrying all sorts of banners and flags. It was Sheridan. He wore a

> slouched hat, a common army blouse, and pants tucked inside his cavalry boots. He wore a belt, but neither sword, pistol, nor significance of rank was visible about him, and carried a short, substantial riding whip…. He raised in his stirrups, leaned forward, and peered down through the gathering twilight towards the advancing enemy…. There was something positively startling in his appearance … a fiendish anticipation.

He told the 1st Maine "Well, boys, you've had rough works this afternoon, but damn 'em, I'll drill 'em for you to-morrow."[103]

As the enemy approached, Sheridan, Custer, and attending staff officers rode along the Union line, drawing enemy fire. Among the casualties was "an enthusiastic reporter of the New York Herald who was shot in the shoulder [while] following the general."*[104]

Despite the blue line of troopers and the artillery fire, the Confederates were confident: "[A]bout sun set when the Enemy made a stand and gave us a warm reseption but not withstanding the grape and canister was flying thick and minny bauls fawling as thick as hale we marched forwards to meat the Enemy at the Point of our good old Sotheran bayonetts."[105]

As Pickett's men advanced in the near-darkness across the open plain, the horse artillery opened fire. An observer recalled that "every time the guns were discharged the grape swept that part of the line completely away, and the line would wheel into column and fill up the gap just vacated, only to meet the same fate…. There was nothing to prevent the artillery from recharging and firing, and therefore each man knowly stepped into a dead man's shoes. It was an act of suicide."[106] The long line of infantry steadily advanced. "We used to think that living was such a poor life with them that they did not much care to continue it," wrote a Union soldier. "They had an air of abandon, a sort of

---

*Charles A. Humphreys wrote that "This daring ride of Sheridan drew an increasing blaze of musketry along the enemy's advancing line, and it emptied several saddles of the dashing cavalcade; and it wounded Theodore Wilson, a too venturesome reporter of the New York Herald, an incident which Sheridan long years after recalled to me with some glee, as he felt that the reporter was out of place."[111]

The view looking northwest from the area of Sheridan's breastworks. Pickett's Confederate infantry attacked across these open fields at twilight, but was repulsed by Sheridan's guns (photograph by the author).

devil-may-care swing in their long stride as they advanced over [the] field."[107]

The men behind the barricades lay still until Pickett's troops were within short range. They opened fire, with "Custer's repeating rifles pouring out such a shower of lead that nothing could stand up against it."[108]

But the Confederates stood and returned the fire. A witness recalled that "I saw volleys fired at Copeland's and Pennington's brigades of such extent as to make a perfect sheet of lead. It seemed as if no man within the range could escape, and the eyes of lookers on were turned to the line as each succeeding volley was fired, expecting to see the ground covered with killed and wounded. Fortunately most of the volleys were fired too high."[109]

Long rows of rifles from both sides spat flame for the next few minutes, until it became too dark to see. "Gradually the fire from the enemy became fitful and irregular, and soon ceased all together," recalled a soldier behind the barricade. "The fight was short. The darkening hours of night now closed the murderous work."[110]

Pickett

The Confederate soldiers were disappointed at the order to halt for the night. "We had every reason to suppose that we were on the eve of completing a victory, when we were halted in front of Dinwiddie Courthouse," wrote an incredulous officer.

Major Matthew H. Cryer, 6th Ohio Cavalry (Ohio Historical Society).

day had ended with a terrible cost for some regiments. Barringer's North Carolina brigade had suffered nearly 50 percent casualties, and only two field officers were left in his three regiments; within Company H, 5th North Carolina Cavalry, every man except the captain had been killed or wounded. One Confederate recalled finding 27 bullet holes in his clothing and rucksack. Losses were relatively light in Rosser's and Pickett's Divisions—the 17th Virginia Infantry's count of 40 men killed, captured, or wounded was the highest loss in the infantry. Total Confederate losses can only be estimated at about 800–900 men.

Early in the morning Pickett learned that Federal infantry was coming up on his left flank to reinforce Sheridan. Pickett ordered his troops to fall back to their breastworks at Five Forks. This news was even more disturbing and confusing to the exhausted men: they already felt they had been halted unnecessarily on the verge of victory, and had been looking forward to overrunning the Union line at dawn; now they were trudging back to Five Forks at four o'clock in the morning.

Pickett's force camped on the battlefield among the enemy's dead and wounded, about a hundred yards from the Union line. Volunteers retraced the ground until well after midnight, looking for the wounded in the darkness. "We made them as comfortable as we could in the absence of our medical attendants," wrote a volunteer. "[We] made fires, brought water."[111]

Soldiers wandered from fire to fire looking for their regiments. The grim reality of casualty counts began. The

Sheridan

It was a confusing night on the Union side as well, with men looking for commands, and officers looking for men. Expecting a dawn attack, Sheridan forbade the lighting of fires along the line. The night was chilly and cold, and most of the men could not sleep. It made matters worse that

> the rebels ... had built up rousing great fires, around which they were moving, singing, yelling & shouting until near midnight, we could hear the sound of their voices plain.... [We] could see them busily getting supper.... By midnight the fires of the enemy were mostly but a tinkel, a few still burned bright, flaring up every once in a while, showing it had been replenished & a figure could be seen moving about.[112]

Another veteran recalled that "in the night we heard a great noise, and we expected a night attack; but it did not come, to our great surprise. We could hear what they said—the teamster's exclamations to their horses."[113]

Sheridan had lost about 400 men—killed, wounded, or missing. The 1st Maine Cavalry in Smith's brigade suffered the most, counting 15 killed, 74 wounded, and 6 missing at day's end. Major Matt Cryer, 6th Ohio Cavalry, remembered that

> I was sent for to report in person to General Smith. After commenting on the action of the Regiment with much praise, he said there must be a great mistake in the report of the casualties, as it only gave 17 killed, wounded, and missing.... He ordered me to go to each company and see that the roll was called, and report again in person. I went over

each company, with its orderly examining each man as he was getting much needed sleep, but did not awaken any.... We found one more man who had got back to his company.... So [when] I reported back to General Smith ... he asked for an explanation of how we managed to come out so well. All I could say was that the officers were careful not to expose themselves or the men when it was not absolutely necessary.[114]

Volunteers labored long into the night to gather the Union dead and wounded. The wounded were loaded into "box- and flat-cars, crowded to the utmost limit, and run over a military railroad, a track laid on top of the ground without grading, to City Point. The method of braking at that time was crude, and as we went up and down hill the train would jerk and crash together with such force that the men would slide together on the bottom of the cars."[115]

The night was spent digging and improving the works, and "were now fit to resist horse, foot, or dragoons," wrote one cavalryman. Another remembered that

> Not a loud word, no fire, no noise of any kind was allowed at our breastworks, which we labored at most all night.... We built it about 2 ft. high, but we could have been flanked out of it in 5 min. The night was cold, with slight frost, & we suffered bitterly. We could not move around briskly, it made too much noise, & if we laid down, it was dreadful cold on the wet ground & no cover.[116]

Sheridan wrote to General Grant from a little cabin filled with his wounded men: "This force is too strong for us. I will hold out at Dinwiddie C. H. until I am compelled to leave."[117]

By 10 o'clock that night General Warren's infantry and additional cavalry under General Mackenzie were ordered by Grant to move immediately to Sheridan's support. Both Grant and Sheridan realized Pickett was in a dangerous position, out of his works and isolated. At three in the morning Sheridan wrote to Warren that

> you are in rear of the enemy's line and almost on his flank. I will hold on here…. Attack at daylight anyhow, and I will make an effort to get the road … and if I do, you can capture the whole lot of them…. Do not fear my leaving here. If the enemy remains, I shall fight at daylight.[118]

Warren had had a rough time of it as well on Sheridan's right—he attacked Lee's works in the Battle of the White Oak Road the same afternoon, and had been driven back in disorder. The first of Warren's men did not appear until 7:30 in the morning on April 1.

April 1, 1865

Pickett

The exhausted Confederates were roused, and the first of the infantry trudged back to Five Forks about three in the morning, followed by the cavalry. A soldier complained that we "found ourselves in a road along which our whole force, cavalry, infantry, and artillery were moving. All movements now bore the aspect of a hurried retreat…. The roads were terribly bad. It was with the greatest difficulty the ambulances

and ordnance wagons could be moved along."[119]

Wounded comrades continued to be picked up along the way. General W. P. Roberts, one of Barringer's brigade commanders, wrote that "I distinctly remember that after the Battle of Chamberlain's Run, I passed the regiment [the 1st North Carolina Cavalry] on the road, and its great loss both in splendid officers and gallant men made such an impression upon me that I wept like a child."[120]

By 10 o'clock in the morning Pickett's force was safely behind its massive log barriers at Five Forks. Later that morning Pickett received the following message from Robert E. Lee:

> Hold Five Forks at all hazards. Protect road to Ford's Depot and prevent Union forces from striking the Southside Railroad. Regret exceedingly your forced withdrawal, and your inability to hold the advantage you had gained.[121]

In the afternoon, Generals Pickett, Munford, and Rosser left the front to attend a shad bake on Hatcher's Run a few miles in the rear of their defenses.

Sheridan

When dawn broke the battlefield was hidden in fog. The quiet, expectant Union line could not see the enemy in their front. The crossroads of Dinwiddie Courthouse was jammed with men and wagons, and "the venerable court house had been sacked, and both recent and ancient documents were scattered over the ground in every direction."[122] As the fog lifted, Generals Sheridan,

Custer, and Merritt and a flock of Union staff officers rode forward and peered through the haze at a moving body of men. One of the staff recalled that

> They were in our immediate front, and we heard chopping distinctly. I was the officer sent out in presence of General Sheridan himself to develop the line which he thought was General Warren's; and I found that it was the enemy that I received the fire personally from; a line of infantry—a long skirmish line in the edge of the woods, representing a large force as I supposed.[123]

Sheridan was keenly disappointed that Pickett was escaping, and incensed that Warren's infantry had not yet arrived. The opportunity to "roll Pickett up" was lost.

The men were mobilized and moved out in pursuit. "We advanced over the same ground lost the night before," stated John Clark of the 7th Michigan Cavalry. "They [were] retiring before us & [we] were surprised to see the number of dead Rebs & few Yanks."[124] The two forces were close enough for continual light skirmishing, with the Confederate rear guard firing from trees, barns, and fences to slow down the Union pursuit. As the Union soldiers moved northward toward Five Forks, they captured the Confederate wounded in the field hospitals that had been set up in houses and barns on the west side of Chamberlain's Run.

The Battle of Five Forks

Sheridan approached the Confederate works at Five Forks in the mid-afternoon, and was anxious to get infantry in place for the assault. Warren himself had finally appeared, it was getting late, and Sheridan wanted the Union victory by nightfall. (As nightfall had aided him the day before, he did not want Pickett to have the same opportunity to escape defeat). Both Sheridan and Grant were irritated with Warren's inclination to procrastinate, and relieved him of command prior to the start of the battle. The Confederate commanders were still attending the shad bake when the Union troops stormed the log and earth defenses at dusk. The fighting was furious, brutal, and hand-to-hand. Pickett arrived too late to be effective. The Confederates broke and retreated, with a heavy loss in killed and wounded, and thousands captured. The battered Confederate cavalry fought a skillful delaying action that allowed the infantry to escape.

When he heard the news General Robert E. Lee wrote to General J. C. Breckenridge, the Secretary of War:

> It is absolutely necessary that we should abandon our position tonight or run the risk of being cut off in the morning. I have given all the orders to officers on both sides of the river, and have taken every precaution that I can to make the movement successful. It will be a difficult operation, but I hope not impracticable.[125]

The Battle of Five Forks was the breakthrough Union victory Grant was hoping for, and the Confederate army was in full retreat. It was a running fight for the next nine days, until the exhausted and starving Confederate forces surrendered on April 9, 1865. The Civil War was over.

Conclusions

Over 130 years have passed since the Battle of Dinwiddie Courthouse was fought. Official reports, accounts, reminiscences, memoirs, and accusations and denials, many of them clouded by age, are the surviving records of this battle. From today's neutral historical distance it is easy to criticize and judge performance in combat. What is lost to the historian is the fear, mayhem, exhaustion, and lack of communication that shaped men's actions on that day.

Confederate

There is no question that George Pickett had a difficult job—he had arrived at Five Forks at sunset on March 30 and had to attack the following morning. His men were cold, wet, and exhausted. His cavalry was not fully assembled until after dawn on March 31, and there is a possibility that he did not know Rosser was going to "be up" until his men were on the move.

Accounts about Pickett's battle plan differ—one indicates that Pickett had started out advancing in full strength down the road toward Dinwiddie Courthouse. Then, probably with a stick in the dirt, the flanking maneuver across Chamberlain's Run was conceived and executed (possibly prompted by the arrival of Rosser's cavalry).

Regardless of its origin, his plan became cumbersome and slow-moving, and about half a day was needed for Pickett's troops to get into position. He

was attempting a flanking maneuver across unknown country, even with a local guide—he at least knew the country in his front at Five Forks. Chamberlain's Creek had apparently not been scouted, and the resistance there was a surprise.

Fitz Lee apparently understood most the importance of taking Fitzgerald Ford, and was probably counting on the infantry he knew was coming behind him. His decision to attack the ford was the best one of the day by any Confederate or Union commander. Had his men held the ford, they would have established a defensible crossing point, and Pickett's men could have swarmed across under less deadly fire. But even support from other cavalry units failed (bad communications between commanders, and some decisions made in the interest of self-preservation), and brave men were needlessly sacrificed. Had timely support arrived, Pickett would have crossed about noon, and the fight would have been finished well before dark. The advance could have been quick enough that Custer would not have made it in time to save Sheridan, and Pickett would have scored a sparkling victory.

Pickett's conclusion that Fitzgerald Ford could not be crossed is perplexing. Why couldn't the infantry and artillery cross there, when the cavalry had already waded it once, and would do so again? Pickett could have at least left some of his reserves at the creek to support the attack. The enemy had been bloodied, and a vigorously renewed attack would have likely forced the crossing. Instead, Pickett wasted two hours looking for another place to cross, which gave the Federal forces time to think, and strengthen defenses. This peculiar inde-cisiveness (perhaps born of too much worry about the safety of his men) affected his judgment during the battle.

The battle could still have been a Confederate victory if Barringer, Beales, and Lee had overcome their dread and crossed their cavalry at Fitzgerald Ford in the early afternoon as first ordered. It is likely they would have reached Sheri-dan's position before it was entrenched, and with more daylight left to carry the fight.

Once the attack was moving and underway, the Confederates were halted at sunset, when many of the soldiers were confident they would sweep over the enemy (even Sheridan admitted this "force is too strong for us"). This was the final opportunity for Pickett to score a victory.

The Confederate artillery had no effect during the battle, and spent most of the day hauling itself between Fitzgerald and Danse's Fords. With the exception of lobbing some shells during the second crossing of Chamberlain's Run, the Confederate artillery was not used where it was needed most: the twi-light assault on Sheridan's defensive line.

Yet even if the Confederates had taken Dinwiddie Courthouse, they would have been shattered the follow-ing day by Sheridan's reinforced com-mand, either at Dinwiddie Courthouse or later, at Five Forks. So Pickett's de-cision to withdraw to Five Forks was prudent; his absence on the field the following day absolutely inexcusable. A Confederate victory at Dinwiddie Courthouse would have had no bearing on the outcome of the war—only on the glory of those who fought it.

Sheridan

Despite his extra day of scouting and rest (a luxury denied Pickett), Sheridan did not appear to have any par-ticular plan on the 31st. Several of his officers indicated they had been simply ordered to do more reconnaissance. Sheridan knew where Pickett was—his patrols had found him the day before. Yet he only mobilized Devins forward, much as he had done the previous day. Unlike his recent fevered talk of being ready to "go about smashing things," Sheridan was being uncharacteristically timid. If he had conceived a battle plan and advanced at dawn, he would have stripped the initiative from Pickett. Sheridan should have had sound knowl-edge of the area through his active scouting patrols, and with his control of the fords, could have launched his own flanking attack on Pickett. A hard as-sault on Pickett in the morning could have possibly turned Warren's defeat at the Battle of White Oak Road into a re-sounding victory, sending the Confed-erate Army into flight a day sooner.

Once engaged, Sheridan performed well and had a good sense of what was happening on the field. He responded well to situations as they developed, and his clear thinking allowed his units to fall back to a well-organized defensive line. Sheridan used his reserve forces effectively (unlike Pickett), and enjoyed very good performances from most of his brigade commanders, especially Smith (again, unlike Pickett).

The regimental histories are filled with references to valiant stands, firing until the enemy was only 15 paces away, and "galling fire." Take for example the

8th Pennsylvania Cavalry during the Gregg-Gibbs flank attack on Pickett's right: "[We faced] a murderous fire, losing very heavily, but, after a fight at very close quarters, drove the enemy from the woods. We were soon attacked by overwhelming numbers ... and forced to fall back." During the entire day the regiment lost only three men killed and 12 wounded. This kind of fighting would have produced high casualties and captured men—yet most of these regiments had light losses. This indicates that for them the fight was basically a heavy, running skirmish all afternoon. Only a few regiments, such as the 1st Maine Cavalry, were dangerously exposed in serious combat.

Aftermaths: Confederate

A Meeting After the War

Colonel William H. Cheek commanded the First North Carolina Cavalry, and led both charges across Chamberlain's Creek against Smiths's brigade, including the 1st Maine Cavalry. He later recalled a chance reunion with an officer from that regiment that "showed the reputation of [my] regiment in the camp of the enemy":

> In Washington City on my return home from Johnson's Island Prison in August 1865, [I found myself in a] room ... crowded with Federal officers, all of course strangers to me. Feeling very lonely, and wishing to have someone to talk with, I determined to make an acquaintance. Seeing an officer of commanding appearance, with an open,

approachable face, clad in cavalry uniform, with the insignia of a colonel, I went up to him and introduced myself as a late Colonel of the First North Carolina Cavalry. He grasped my hand most cordially and soon called up and introduced quite a number of other officers. He told them "I have the honor of having met Col. Cheek once before. It was on the 11th of May last, at a little place called Goodall's tavern about eighteen miles from Richmond. On that occasion Col. Cheek, with his regiment, the First North Carolina Cavalry, which was considered the best regiment of cavalry on his side, met the First Maine, which held a similar reputation on our side. I saw these two fine regiments come hand-to-hand, in open field, with drawn sabres. The clash was terrific, the fighting was furious and obstinate, but the First Maine was driven from the field. An officer of the First Maine, after the surrender, speaking of his regiment, made the proud boast that it was never driven from the field but once during the war, but, said he, we consider that no disgrace or reflection, for it was done by the First North Carolina."[126]

A Confederate at Grant's Headquarters

Confederate soldier J. D. Hodges fell to the ground from the concussion of an artillery shell in the late afternoon, and was left for dead. When he regained consciousness, he found he had been captured by Federal soldiers:

> Night came on with hundreds of others being conducted to the rear of the Union army; I got cold almost beyond endurance because of my wet clothes. I arrived at General Grant's headquarters about 10 o'clock at night. Although I had begged my Yankee guards for water, it was not until I reached Grant's

headquarters that I was satisfied. There was a young Union soldier posting a relief guard. I could hardly speak, I was chattering so from the cold, but I asked him for a drink. "Stay here," said the young Union soldier, "till I post this relief and I'll get you some water." In a short time he came to me and said: "Come with me." I followed him to his tent where he had a good fire. He gave me water to drink and bade me sit down and warm myself. During the warming process he plied me with many and varied questions: "How many men has Lee these days?" "What sort of rations?" "What morale of the army?" "When are they going to surrender?" etc. Well, I was too proud and loyal to tell him what I really thought. I painted in roseate colors everything from the Confederate standpoint. "The army's never been in better condition." "The people never more determined." "No end to the war until complete separation is effected," etc.

Confederate private J. D. Hodges, 5th North Carolina Cavalry (North Carolina Division of Archives and History).

The Union soldier replied: "I know, my young friend, that you do not believe half you have said. I see that you have too much intelligence not to know that the end is near. Lee will have surrendered in less than ten days from this day.

But somehow I admire you and your pluck and spirit. Upon one condition, I am going to let you stay with me in this tent all night—promise me that you will not try to get away—you cannot get away, if you try. But you must promise me to not try."

. "I am not so sure that I could not get away," I replied. "As a scout, I have traveled all through this section of the country, but I will assure you that I will not abuse your kindness. I pledge you on the honor of a Confederate soldier—I have nothing else to pledge and nothing else more valuable anywhere—that I will not try to get away." He then took a sheepskin off of his cot and laid it down, and told me to make a pillow of my coat that had become dry by his good warm fire by that time, and, in perfect abandon, I slept the sweetest sleep I had had in many a day. All too soon and before I had aroused from the first snooze, he touched me on the shoulder, saying, "It's getting light; you must get back." As we were going back to where the other Confederates were under guard, he noted that I had on my person something that he wanted—something that was never seen in the Union army, but was common with some Confederates. He wanted it, he said, as a war relic. He offered money for it. I said: "No, you have been so good to me that I want you to accept it as a present from one in token of my appreciation and friendship."

"I will not have it unless you let me pay for it."

"Then have it your way," I said.

The exchange was made. Then putting me in among the other prisoners, he said "Good-by Johnnie," and I said, "Good-by, Yank."

Then we parted, never to see each other, never to hear from each other again. A thousand times I have thought of him. Many times I have dreamed of him. A thousand times I have told my people the happenings of that eventful night…. I am now eighty-five and feeble, but I would travel across a continent to see him again.[127]

Death of a Brother

Private R. G. Barlow, a member of Pickett's 32nd Virginia Infantry, wrote about the death of his brother, William Henry Barlow, and Adjutant Pettit, one of their officers. His brother fell during the surprise attack on the Confederate right flank early in the afternoon by Gibbs's and Gregg's Brigades:

[We were] in line of battle, at the time, charging Sheridan's Cavalry [Davies's men, most notably the 1st New Jersey Cavalry], who were dismounted. In this charge he was shot & fell. I was immediately behind him, as he fell, I seized his musket, (mine having failed to fire, I broke the stoke off) & continued in the fight. We were in a little while, driven back a short distance, about 200 or 300 yards—when we were retired Adjt. Pettit was killed, while Colonel Montague was trying to reform the front (the Enemy had overlapped us on the right). The Yankey Soldier who killed Adjt Pettit was immediately shot (literally riddled with bullets) by order of Col. Montague. It was in a hand to hand conflict. The soldier who shot Pettit was within ten ft. of him.

Our command soon reformed, & being reinforced by Stuart's brigade, renewed the charge and drove the enemy to Dinwiddie C. H. in their breast works…. In the Second Charge referred to above I passed over my brothers body again & when our command halted for the night, I obtained permission to go after Henry. I found him dead—shot through the left hand & the stomach. I covered him up with his blanket. He must have been in the act of firing when he was shot; He was buried next morning on the field where killed.[128]

Raised from the Dead

During the second crossing of Chamberlain's Run, Colonel Cheek of the First North Carolina Cavalry mentioned standing waist-deep in the water as he conferred with Lieutenant Colonel William H. Cowles when Cowles was shot in the head. Cheek saved him from drowning and sent the badly wounded officer to the rear.

Cowles was a popular officer, and his loss saddened his men greatly. His wound was regarded as mortal, and he had been placed in a field hospital behind the lines during the night. Fred Foard, an officer from the 1st North Carolina, recalled that

a minie-ball ploughed across his skull, a little above mid-way from the upper tip of the ear to the top of his head, making a furrough in which one could have buried one's fore-finger. He was taken to a dwelling house in rear of our line of battle out of gun-shot that had been converted into a field hospital. The surgeons after careful examination pronounced him dead and ordered him taken to a room assigned to the dead in which there were already many corpses.

Lieutenant Colonel William H. Cowles, 1st North Carolina Cavalry (North Carolina Division of Archives and History).

The next morning when we were marching by, Chris Burchett, Colonel Cowles' faithful Orderly, bethought him that the little articles of intimate personal use on Colonel Cowles' body would be cherished mementos to his aged father and sister. The Orderly went into the room among the dead and took various articles from his pockets. Colonel Cowles also wore a watch attached to a black silk cord that went over his head to remove which it was necessary to lift the upper part of his body. The motion caused a deep groan from the supposed dead man. It was then about nine o'clock in the morning. He had been there since four o'clock the preceding afternoon among the dead, without showing a sign of life.... He soon revived sufficiently to be placed in an ambulance to be taken to a hospital in Petersburg, 20 miles away.

The ambulance was captured by the enemy but the desperately wounded man was ... skillfully treated and after a long convalenscence, he ultimately recovered.

His right arm was permanently paralyzed, but though without apparent impairment of the General vigor of his constitution.... He learned to write with his left hand and I have seen him knock a squirrel out of the top of a tall oak tree, shooting with his Colt's Army Six from his left hand.[129]

Postwar Hauntings

The Adams house offered temporary shelter to the skirmishers from the 2nd Ohio Cavalry, as they tried to delay Pickett's advance from the woods in the late afternoon. Originally built about 1800, it still stands today. When the house was renovated in the late 1800s and early 1900s, numerous bullets and artillery shells were removed from its walls. Former residents talk about shadows without sources, and a strange rubbing noise. The most recent tenant reported she had heard this noise also, and that it sounded familiar. Despite going through the entire house, she could not locate the source. A few weeks later she attended a flea market, and met a man who inquired where she lived. When she told him, he said he had lived in that house too. He paused, looked at her, and asked her matter-of-factly if she had heard the "wagon wheels." She immediately realized that the familiar sounds she had heard were "wagon wheels moving on stones." The Adams house was behind the Confederate line at dark, and within Federal lines the following morning. Wagons would have likely moved

wounded or dying soldiers to and from the building.

Aftermaths: Federal

Death of a Father

When preparing to fight on foot, cavalrymen count off by fours, and every fourth man holds horses for the previous three men and himself. Hugo Mullert of the 10th New York Cavalry, Davies's brigade, was holding horses during the early afternoon when Pickett had crossed Danses's Ford. The dismounted troopers moved into the woods, and "we watched every noise that came from the direction in which our men had disappeared." The firing intensified, and wounded men began to stagger through the woods. Eventually all became confusion. As Mullert led his fractious and wounded horses further to the rear, he met

a boy in Bugler's uniform.... I recognized him; it was "Eddy," the son of the Captain of Co. H. He was weeping, and asked me for water. On my inquiring whether he was wounded, he said: "No, but my father; there he lies!" He stepped to the side of the road a little way and pointed to the ground.... Under a little dogwood tree, stretched on the grass to die, lay the Captain, a man of about 35 or 40 years. His youngest son, who was down on his knees by his right side weeping and bathing his fathers face, was held by the latter in his right arm, while the left hand pressed on his chest, as if he were in great pain.

I dismounted quickly and gave him a drink. Leaving my canteen with them, I hurried to the field hospital, which

I found close by, for assistance. The Captain had, no doubt, after being wounded, tried to reach the hospital by aid of his children, who were with him in the field, but strength failing, he lay down under this pretty dogwood, just for a while.[130]

Sheridan's Chief of Scouts

In 1864 General Phil Sheridan formed a group of professional scouts, commanded by Major Henry H. Young, a 22-year-old officer from the 2nd Rhode Island Infantry. Young had been noticed by his superiors for his brave actions and quick thinking ever since the Battle of First Manassas, which had won him a promotion to first lieutenant. A cavalryman remembered that

Young's men dressed in the Confederate uniform habitually, mingled with the people, told them the news and got the news of them in return, cursed the Yankees, and drank stirrup-cups of apple-jack to their discomfiture, warned the host against their coming, and then rode away, while one of the number quickly slipped back through unfrequented paths and communicated the latest from the front to the general command. At night, while the troops rested, Young and his men would be miles away in every direction.[131]

Young is perhaps best remembered for his daring capture of Confederate Major Harry Gilmor inside Confederate lines in 1864. Sheridan grew to rely on Young's information. During the advance on Dinwiddie Courthouse, Young's men were everywhere, traveling the backroads at night and talking with the local residents. A cavalry officer wrote that

I had just lain down when an orderly awoke me; in response to the call I found they had halted about twenty mounted men, dressed mostly in Confederate uniforms. The officer in command carried an order from General Sheridan to pass them through the lines, but the officer on picket was not quite sure that it was the thing to do with such a motley crew…. I soon found that they were Sheridan's scouts under command of Major Young and no further questions were asked.[132]

Two days after the battle of Five Forks, Young captured General Rufus Barringer, Colonel William H. Cheek, and several other staff officers in an accidental confrontation. Cheek remembered that "Major Young rode with me back to his camp, and I found him to be a pleasant, entertaining and considerate gentleman…. He did me [a] great favor. It was reported all through our army that I was killed a few days before. Fearing that this report might reach my wife, I told this to Major Young and he seemed to sympathize with me and was anxious to assist." Young ordered him to write a letter, which was personally delivered by a Union soldier to Mrs. Cheek's door.[133]

In a letter to E. M. Stanton dated April 19, Sheridan wrote that

I desire to make special mention of the valuable service of Major Henry H. Young, 2nd Rhode Island Infantry, chief of my scouts, during the cavalry expedition from Winchester, Virginia, to the James River. His personal gallantry and numerous conflicts with the enemy won the admiration of the

whole command. In the late campaign from Petersburg to Appomatox Courthouse he kept me constantly informed of the movements of the enemy and brought in prisoners from brigadier generals on down. The information gained through him was invaluable. I earnestly request that he be made a lieutenant-colonel by brevet.[134]

After the Civil War, Young and some men, under Sheridan's orders, crossed into Mexico to assist the regime of Mexican President Benito Juarez in its fight against the French. Young and his small patrol were ambushed by a band of ex-Confederates and Mexican renegades. He was shot from his horse in the Rio Grande River, and his body never recovered.

Late-Afternoon Rescue

Lieutenant Leander L. Comins of Company A, First Maine Cavalry, was struck by a bullet as he helped direct the retreat after the Confederates' successful crossing of Chamberlain's Run. Three men went back to find him "moaning upon the ground, the pine needles about him besprinkled and splashed by his blood as he had crawled and writhed about in his agony. Two rifles were thrown upon the ground and the lieutenant placed across them." A volley of musketry from advancing skirmishers killed one of the rescuers, and Comins was again wounded.

J. D. Waller, of the 32nd Virginia Infantry, recalled that "we had advanced but a short distance when I saw a squad of Federals a few rods in our front, bearing a wounded man from the field. Some of my men fired; I shouted 'For Shame, don't shoot wounded men,' and then shouted to the Federals, 'Take him on Yanks; we all won't fire,' not thinking it possible for them to escape capture."

A nearby Maine officer quickly dismounted his horse, and Lieutenant Comins was put in the saddle. The Confederates followed closely with cries of "Wounded man on the horse, don't shoot him", "don't shoot, look out, men, don't hurt the man on the horse," which were taken up by many Confederate voices as they continued to push the retreating Federals. One of Comins's rescuers wrote "there were five hundred or more Confederates following us not half rifle range away, who seemed to have taken our party under their special protection."

Lieutenant Comins was delirious, and randomly shouted out orders, addressed loved ones, and repeated a stanza from an old hymn. Blood dripped from his overflowing boot. He begged to be laid down so the others could escape, but was told the Confederates were not firing at them. A man with him wrote that he said, "What! Not firing at us?" Then his crushed thigh made him groan, and [he] settled forward upon the horse's mane and uttered his last words on field of battle—"God help us," and "Thank them, thank them for..."—them meaning the enemy undoubtedly. Ten

Opposite: **Major Henry H. Young, chief of scouts for General Phil Sheridan (U.S. Army Military History Institute).**

minutes later we were within our lines behind the guns on the Dinwiddie plateau.

Lieutenant Comins died ten days later.[135]

Premonitions

The 2nd Ohio Cavalry had just arrived on the field in the late afternoon, and was preparing to advance toward the Adams house to delay the Confederate infantry. After counting off by fours, Sergeant Francis S. Finch dismounted and told his friends he had gone through four years of war and never been hurt, but "that he was going to get it this time." Worried horse-holders offered to switch with Finch. He replied "No, sir, it is my place to go, and I shall go!" Finch, and the others, held the house for a few minutes, delivering hot repeater fire that opened gaps in the Confederate ranks. When the Confederates unleashed the thundering volley of musketry that rattled the house, Sergeant Finch fell with a bullet in his thigh. He was carried from the field during the retreat a few minutes later, but bled to death from the severed artery in his leg.[136]

Opposite: **Lieutenant Leander L. Comins, 1st Maine Cavalry (Tobie,** *History of the First Maine Cavalry***).**

II

"I'll Live Yet to Dance on That Foot!": The Civil War Experiences of Colonel Charles Blacknall, 23rd North Carolina Infantry

Introduction

Like most Confederate officers during the Civil War, Charles C. Blacknall was a wealthy, well-educated farmer and slave-owner. Unquestionably forthright, opinionated, self-confident, and energetic, he typically led those who surrounded him—family members, friends, business associates, and soldiers.

A prolific writer, he sent many letters home to friends and family during his service in the Confederate army from 1861–1864. Typescripts of these letters survive in the North Carolina Archives

in Raleigh (all quotations are from these letters or other source material in the O. W. Blacknall Papers unless otherwise cited). Written by a man who loved words, this collection is a dramatic yet accurate portrayal of every aspect of an officer's life.[1]

Blacknall hated the drudgery of camp life and drilling, and was occasionally embarrassed by the commanding general during "lessons and tactics." He longed for the front. His regiment, the 13th North Carolina Infantry (later the 23rd) arrived by train a day late for the First Battle of Manassas, and the rest of 1861 was spent in camp. The regiment fought well at The Seven Days Battles in 1862. Blacknall was captured the following year at Chancellorsville, and wounded seriously at Gettysburg. He was later imprisoned at Johnson's Island. Wounded in the ankle at the Battle of Winchester in 1864, he refused to let surgeons amputate, vowing to "live to dance" on the foot. The Confederate surgeons left him to be captured by the Federals, who nursed him tenderly in a Winchester home until he died of complications two months later.

Blacknall's letters detail his relationship with his family members, and their hardships during his absence. His vanity also comes into play, especially regarding his wounds. Because he is such an honest man in his letters and expresses his feelings, the reader can witness the man change as he becomes consumed by the war.

The Early Years (1830–1860)

Charles Christopher Blacknall was born to Thomas and Caroline Blacknall on December 4, 1830. The following year the family moved to their residence at "Beech Spring," near the town of Kittrell in Granville County. Thomas died shortly thereafter, and the widow Caroline raised her three sons (George, Charles, and Henry) there for the next 20 years.

Caroline, the "embodiment of prudence and economy," devoted herself to the education and careful upbringing of her children. Charles received his first schooling from his mother and later attended the country schools in the neighborhood. His son Oscar recalled that

> from a very tender age [my father] manifested the quickness of apprehension, clearness and command of faculty, power of concentration and retentiveness of memory which characterized him as a man. When only four years old he was taken to the [commencement] of Mr. Young's school ... on the road to Oxford. When the speaking was over it was found he could repeat considerable portions of the orations of every scholar that had spoken. This so surprised and pleased the crowd that when the ceremonies at the school house were all over, they took him to Patton's store hard by, placed him on the counter and bade him hold forth. Not a whit abashed he acquitted himself so well that "four punces" and "six punces" [coins] were rained upon him.

A quick and eager student, at 16 Charles was placed in a private academy in Henderson, where he excelled in Latin and mathematics. He was a voracious reader and especially delighted in poetry. His outdoor skills included swimming, hunting, and riding. Charles pursued all his interests with a tireless vigor, including his meals. "He delighted in plain fare," wrote Oscar, "[and] was always a very fast eater; so much so that he began to suffer at an early age from dyspepsia. The unwisdom and unpoliteness of fast eating he was fully alive to, but breaking himself of it he never could, owing to his temperament which forced him to do all things quickly or not at all."

Following graduation Charles experimented with clerking and teaching school. In 1850 he left for Rome, Georgia, to study law. When his mother learned he was about to marry the instructor's daughter, she sent her son Henry to fetch him back, and he dutifully returned to North Carolina. The following year found Charles as a gentleman farmer, managing an uncle's estate near Kittrell.

It was in 1851 that he was introduced to Virginia Spencer, "a dark brunette ... [who wore] her hair in long curls after the fashion of the day. Her eyes were fine and brown, but wore ever a slight shadow of sadness." They courted briefly before marrying on October 16, 1851. Afterwards the wedding procession drove to Beech Spring, where an elegant dinner reception was held. As the guests began to depart

> [Virginia's] mother made ready to return to her home, [and] the bride decided that she must go, too! She had never been separated from her mother for a moment. Her mother's remonstrance was in vain. So return ... she did, the groom going with her. The next day they returned to Beech Spring, where they took up their abode.

A few months later Charles turned 21 and received from his mother "very good property in Negroes and money." Two of these slaves were able masons, and were sold by Charles for $4,000 each. In the summer of 1852 Charles and Virginia had a new residence built at Beech Spring, and Oscar, their first child, was born there on September 6, 1852.

The next year the young Blacknall family moved to Franklinton, ten miles from Beech Spring. Charles and his half-cousin, Thomas, founded C. C.

AND T. H. BLACKNALL, which dealt in "dry goods ... and expensive finery." Charles proved to be a good salesman and fine accountant, and the enterprise continued to grow. The owners, however, granted credit too easily and disliked requesting payment on overdue accounts, and profits began to dwindle. They closed the business in 1857, and Charles Blacknall became engaged for the next year in the manufacture of chewing tobacco. Oscar recalled,

> [My father] was intensely fond of letters, but between his business and his friends he had but little time to give books except late at night.... My chief recollection of him [in Franklinton] is tilted back in a chair reading by candlelight interminable pages of large volumes after all the rest of the house was in bed and asleep.

Charles also served as mayor and justice of the peace in Franklinton. He was one of the most respected men in the region and was well known for his fairness and honesty. He enjoyed the attention of others, was a forceful speaker, and invariably became the leader of any group he was involved with. He disdained the use of alcohol. In contrast to his many virtues, he rarely attended church. An almost reckless intensity was evident at an early age,

> when [as] a very small boy he went rabbit hunting in the snow, wearing a new pair of shoes. The shoes hurt his feet so that walking in them became impossible. The snow was deep and the weather exceedingly cold, but ... removing his shoes and hanging them on a limb in the woods, he hunted the whole day barefoot.

Similarly, this bearing carried over to his domestic life and the way he interacted with his family. He welcomed new challenges and prided himself on confronting them in a direct, head-on fashion, and had little patience for indecisiveness or timidness. Oscar wrote,

> My recollection begins with this great snow, I being then four years old. I remember ... that when I begged to go out in the snow, [my father] gratified my wish by taking me to the back door and tossing me into a snow bank some six feet deep. It seemed a mile deep to me and I was greatly frightened. My mother screamed and I was quickly dug out by the servants, an animated snowball, for ears, eyes, mouth and garments were full of snow. My father laughed and said that was the way to make a man of me.

Charles Blacknall embarked on his next enterprise in 1858, when he and his brothers bought the Kittrell's Springs property. The mineral spring had long been known for its curative power, and had gradually grown into a rural summer resort. The Blacknalls began an energetic and expensive transformation of the property, building a stately, four-story hotel complete with grand ballroom, bowling alley, landscaped greens, and graveled walks. The Kittrell's Springs Hotel was opened in 1860, and the resort was at once filled with guests arriving by rail or private carriage.

Charles and his family remained in Franklinton until 1859, when they moved to the Kittrell's Springs resort. By this time Mr. and Mrs. Blacknall were the parents of three sons and one daughter. In June of that year President Buchanan and his entourage visited Franklinton, and Charles, as mayor, was required to deliver a short address of welcome. Due to the large crowd,

> it was necessary to improvise a platform on which [the Mayor] could stand to be seen and heard. The hurry was great. The platform proved insecure. Right in the midst of his speech it gave way, dropping [the Mayor] waist deep in its ruins.... But he showed not the least sign of confusion, continuing his address the moment that the crash was over.

The War Begins

With the imminence of war, Charles Blacknall put aside the management of the "Springs" to raise a company of volunteer soldiers. He wrote

> I may perhaps never have the gratification of viewing [this diary] after the conclusion of the war, as there is no way of telling which way the Yankees may shoot in battle, and some stray ball might suddenly make me "adorn a tale" instead of living to relate it, but ... I am resolved to do my duty and to use what means I can command towards a vigorous prosecution of this unjust and unholy war, in which we have been forced by our unnatural enemies of the North.

Charles was eager for this next challenge and adventure. He traveled across Granville County delivering enthusiastic recruitment speeches and urged the men to defend their homes and families. The company, first named the Granville Rifles, was drilled on the grounds of the hotel, marching and countermarching, with tobacco sticks substituting for rifles on their shoulders. Blacknall's first letter as a Confederate

soldier was addressed to his brother
George on May 27th, 1861:

> While surrounded by the noise and
> confusion of a rollicking crowd of boys
> ... the mind will occasionally steal out of
> the uproar and go back to other days and
> other friends. I think frequently and
> reflect pleasantly upon the many hours
> we have passed together in various and
> sundry ways ... but it seems that fate has
> lifted a mountain between our path-
> ways.... I hope our ways will again come
> together and we be yet once more travel-
> ing along—not as weary pilgrims—but as
> pleasant voyagers upon life's road.... I
> write this amid a tornado of noise and
> confusion and have only to say that camp
> life is more pleasant than you would
> think. All the little inconveniences of
> cooking, etc., drinking Champaign out
> of *tin cups* and eating half cooked food is
> not so annoying as you may suppose.

The Granville Rifles were designated Company G of the 13th Regiment
of North Carolina Volunteers. The ten
companies voted for officers on July 11,
1861. Daniel Harvey Christie, a friend
of Blacknall and the director of the
Henderson Military Institute, was not
well liked by the men of Company G.
Charles wrote to George,

> there was a general consent that I should
> be elected without opposition, our
> County men going for me to a man ...
> but as I am under obligations to Colonel
> Christie and brought him down to
> endeavor to get him a position ... I
> considered that I would be acting in bad
> faith toward him if I permitted my name
> to be used against him. I withdrew with-
> out permitting a ballot to take place and
> urged the Companies to unite on him,
> which they did.

Christie was elected major of the
regiment, and Charles Blacknall was

voted Captain of Company G. Following the elections, the 13th North Carolina Volunteers were mobilized to
Richmond, and were subsequently sent
by train to Manassas Junction. The
troops arrived on July 22, eager to fight,
but soon learned the First Battle of
Manassas had been won the day before
by the Confederate Army. Greatly
affected by the bloody aftermath, Blacknall wrote that the morning was

> dark and lowering and gloomy in the
> extreme, torrents of rain had fallen
> during the night and nature seemed sad
> and mournful.... In every direction you
> behold the dead and dying—sights so
> heartrendering that I turn sorrowfully
> away from them.... Hundreds of men are
> coming in, some in small crowds, others
> alone, stating that their companies are
> entirely lost.... I have read a great deal
> in history about war and battles but I
> can assure you that I had never formed
> the most distant conception of the real-
> ity. I have seen more dead and wounded
> men than I ever expected to see. I see
> many men with their arms or legs shot
> off who seem to be perfectly regardless
> of their loss and as cheerful as if nothing
> had happened.... I had a conversation
> with one of the prisoners and they curse
> old Abe in a hurry for sending them to
> attack us against their will. Some of
> them however talk very brave and say
> that they mean to let us have the worst
> of it yet. Everything in such confusion,
> men rushing in every direction, bringing
> in the dead and wounded, and the
> prisoners, the rain is coming down in
> torrents.... I have already seen more of
> war and its effect than I expected ever to
> witness in a lifetime.

The rest of 1861 proved quiet for
the 13th North Carolina Volunteers.
On July 25th they were assigned to
Colonel Jubal Early's 6th brigade, and

the summer was spent on picket duty in various camps in Virginia. In September they encamped at Union Mills, which served as their base and winter quarters for the rest of the year. In November the designation of the regiment was changed to the 23rd Regiment of North Carolina Troops. The monotony of camp life and the interminable drilling was occasionally broken by short marches and camps for picket duty or other tasks, such as tearing up railroad.

The following excerpts were written by Captain Blacknall during this time period as entries in his journal or letters home to his family. The recipients were his brother George ("Doc"), mother Caroline ("Ma"), Virginia ("Jinnie") his wife, and his son Oscar (nicknamed "Captain"). He occasionally mentions his other children, Charlie, Billie, and Emma. His frustration with dormant camp life is evident in his writings.

Wednesday, July 24th
Our bill of fare today consists of flour (without salt or lard), beef, (which we cannot eat), soap (a very necessary article in camp life, but rather poor as an article of subsistence), vinegar, and candles. So that some of the beauties of soldiering are now being experienced, however we have a cheerful and jovial mess.... We have Major Christie, with his mixture of military and music; Capt. Cheatham with his lectures on morals and science and his puns which supply the place of pepper, salt and spice at dinner; Adjutant Young with his cravings for home and whiskey and his sentiment and song; Lieut Kittrell with his drollery and wit ... Lieut Turner with his pathos and longing after sweet-hearts and sweet-meats ... Lieut Richardson

with his smooth locks and shining face, ready at dinner.... Myself, indiscribable, incomprehensible, that is, so and so, which means that I am, of course, a marvelous proper person in word and thought and preside with considerable gravity and dignity.

Thursday, July 25th
Affairs in camp today—dull and monotonous, time occupied principally in drilling, eating, drilling, studying and reciting Tactics (which by the way I don't at all fancy) eating again and then drilling-drilling, drilling.

Friday, July 26th
Visited the Battle Field ... [riding] in a wagon over the roughest roads perhaps in Christendom. We arrived however without the loss of life or limb on the memorable spot, and found it thronged with hundreds of visitors on a like tour with ourselves, namely sightseeing and I may say with truth that the sights were quite new ... as I had never before viewed the place where "contending nations meet." The ground is yet strewed with countless trophies of the great fight, though the wounded have been removed and cared for by our men (the enemy having basely and ignominiously forsaken their dead & dying) yet the work of interment is still going on and many a poor Yankee yet lies upon the spot where he offered up his life in attempting to invade our soil. We had the pleasure of seeing Genl. Beauregard and staff and many distinguished officers riding over and viewing the field. The General was pointing out with much distinctness the different points of attack and repulse, and stating many interesting incidents connected with the battle.

Sunday, July 28th
Spent the day in lounging around camp which however is some relief from the never-ending drilling, ever-tapping drums and never ceasing, "Forward march," "Right about march," "File right" and left and backwards and forwards and crossways, which constantly

greets my ears, and of which I am heartily tired. But such is the fate of war and a fellow has to know these things in order that he may be able to take care of No. 1 in battle and also that he may do execution when called on.

July 30th
Rain, mud, and Hardee's tactics, disagreeable quite, the tactics being about as clear to my comprehension as the language used at the building of Babel. Didn't know my lesson today at recitation, confound Hardee, but maybe the fault is in me as I did not study the lesson very attentively.

July 31st
Dear Jinnie
I have just received your letter and of course was much pleased to hear from you and the children. This leaves me in good health.... Your precautions in regard to diet &c. are very proper but under the circumstances entirely unnecessary, as I can get nothing but mean Baltimore meat and flour, without lard or anything else.... In regard to dissipation &c. there has not been the least tendency to anything of the kind in the encampment since I have been here. I don't expect there is a thimble full of liquor in the Regiment and the men both officers and privates are so worn out with drilling and moving about, that when they get an hour to rest, they go to sleep & enjoy it. You have no idea of Camp life, in hearing of the enemy's guns, if you think the men are engaged in frolicking and dissipation. The only sound I hear at night is the singing of the soldiers which remind me very much of a camp meeting, together with the roll of the drum and the cry of the sentinel on his post.

August 2, 1861
Dear Captain [Oscar],
I know you will be glad to get a letter from me and so I must write to you, and tell you something about the war and the soldiers.... We all stay in cloth tents and sleep on a bed made of forks driven in

the ground and boards laid on them. The whole country about here is covered with tents and you see nothing but soldiers and guns.... We eat out of tin plates and drink our water out of tin cups, and cook out of doors, sometimes in the rain. I have not seen any families since I left Richmond as there are no women and children about here. I would give as much to see a little boy or a baby as you would give to see Genl. Beauregard. I have seen a great many Yankee prisoners, they look quite mean, after coming here to kill our people and get caught by us. Nearly all the houses in the neighborhood are filled with Yankees who were wounded in the battle.... The cannon sounds very much like thunder only louder and more distinct. You may think it strange that sensible men come together in great armies and shoot each other by the thousand and cause so much suffering in the country. It is indeed strange that they can find no better employment than killing each other. But we know that we have not been the cause of the war and that the Yankees are coming South to kill us and destroy our property and we are compelled in self defense to fight them and we mean to do it ... we will carry on the war until you, and Billy and Charley boy are big enough to come on [and] help us.

August 13, 1861
Dear Ma,
I wrote to you sometime since and have also written frequently to Jinnie and Bro George, but receive very few letters from home.... My health continues good, but I have a good deal of sickness in my company. The morning report shows 30 on the sick list from my Company ... but none of mine are dangerous cases. We have measles principally. I dont know that I ever had them, have I? I am tolerably well pleased with camp life (I have not been inside of a house of any kind in a month) but the duties are very hard and laborious. We rise at light at the tap of the drum, go out and drill an hour and a half or two hours, and a

portion of that in a run, which is the hardest kind of work. We then come in, get breakfast, go out again at 8½ oclock, repeat the same drilling, come in at 10 1/2, then go to officer's recitation and recite 15 or 20 pages in Tactics, which is very complicated and difficult to learn, the lesson being over, we get dinner and at 2 oclock go out to drill and again at 5, remaining till sundown.

August 18, 1861
Dear Jinnie,
I recd your letter a day or two since and was very glad to learn that all was well at home. You must remain where you are and be satisfied until I return (if I ever should) which I hope to do some time before a great while, but I cannot possibly get a furlough now, even if every member of my family was dead I could not get off at present, as the Genl [Beauregard] is refusing everyone.... I [asked] Ma to send me some cakes, but have heard nothing from them. I have not seen anything since I left home but meat & bread, not a particle of fruit of any kind, no vegetables, no watermelons or anything excepting our rations which are quite common and of which I am heartily tired.... We have enough soldiers here to eat up Mr. Eaton's whole crop of corn at one dinner. There is a wonderful difference between my life at present and what it was this time last year. Then I saw nothing but gay people, all seeming to enjoy themselves, now I see sickness, and toil and labor and exposure and privations and hear complaints of all kind about the hardships of war. People who stay at home in comfortable houses and with plenty to eat can form no idea of the life of a soldier. I have seen hundreds of men going for days without a particle of food and sleeping on the ground in a drenching and continual rain, and many of them sick at the same time. My experience will teach me that we can do with one half of the articles which we have heretofore considered necessary and also

that when we are at peace and have plenty to eat we should be happy and satisfied. I am astonished to hear you complain with your lot in life. I know that you and Ma and the children can live well and should be satisfied, for your condition is so much better than one half of the world, you certainly ought rather to rejoice than to complain.

Thursday, August 23rd
Spent the day in looking at the rain fall (and how beautifully it came down). Rode up to the Junction in the evening, read the papers. How they talk about the gallant soldiers, defending the homes and achieving the liberties of the people. Wonder if the Editors ever lived in camp on flour-bread and beef?... Rode by a house this evening—saw the family at supper—all gathered around the table—and the children too—the children—how cheerful and social and homelike it looked, to a soldier, who eats his meals out by the fire.

Sunday, August 26th
We have much sickness in the army around Manassas at present, and many deaths. It is distressing to see men languishing with disease in camp far from home, and from the soothing attentions of a mother, or a female friend. For whatever may be said of women in other respects she is a "ministering angel" around the bed of the sick and the suffering. To die on the field of battle has no terrors, but to linger on a bed of sickness (if there is such a thing in camp as a bed) calls up said reflections and must be peculiarly distressing.

Monday, August 27th
Am officer of the day. My duties are not very onerous, but constant. Such as making rounds among the guard, keeping order generally in camp, and today attempting to suppress a general liquor drinking propensity which seems to prevail in camp, as there is an opportunity (which is highly appreciated by many) to purchase some very mean whiskey at the

moderate price of $1.25 pr quart, from an individual who is sneaking around camp to corrupt and fleece the troops.

Saturday August 31st
In line of battle this morning, hear the roar of cannon in the direction of Alexandria. All are anxious and ready to go forward. Remained all day in bush palaces. Dined today at the Hotel, which is the first time for many weeks that I have eaten anywhere excepting around our own board. Witness a grand tournament between the Generals and commanders at Head quarters, trying their horses at jumping, some lofty falling.

September 14
I am much troubled about the sickness in my Company. We are suffering terribly with measles, pneumonia and Typhoid fever.... I have lost five of my men and have about 25 others on the sick list. Most of them however are improving. Capt Coghill arrived here this morning in much distress. He stopped at Culpeper to see one of his sons that was sent there sick. He found him dead and buried, came on to camp to see a second one who was sick here, found him likewise dead and his third son Wesley sick in bed.

October 4, 1861
Dear Jinnie,
I have written you once or twice in regard to my winter clothes. I will need coat, pants, and two vests ... and such other little things as you may think that I will need. I can procure transportation for [Bro. George] to come and bring the clothing for the soldiers. I sent him some circulars requesting him to hand them around the Ladies and get them to raise us all the articles they could for the winter. We are very comfortable situated while in camp but when the cold weather comes we will necessarily suffer a great deal. Give my love to all our friends and relations, Ma, Uncle Geo, Sallie and the family, and also to the children. I want very much to see them

all and would like to get their pictures, if I cant see them. I expect they will grow out of my knowledge before I see them again. I dont think that I would know Emma now, and I am certain that I have not idea of the looks of the baby [George, born in May 1861]. But Charley Boy and Billy and the Capt. I dont expect will ever change so that I would not know them, even though I was absent a number of years.

Dec. 1st
Dear Ma,
I have nothing whatever to relate that would in the least interest you. Still I consider it my duty to write to you occasionally if it served only to reassure you that I am still mindful of the fact that amid all the trials and vicissitudes of life, all that we are and all the usefullness which we may be able to render in life, is principally owing to the wise instructions of our mothers and to them we owe honor, duty and obedience. We have nothing transpiring in Camp of importance ... all is still in doubt and the future as unknown in regard to the probabilities of a fight at this point, as it has been for the last several months. Our Generals are expecting an attack every day. Tomorrow we will have a grand review of the army. Genls Johnston & Beauregard will present the battle flags to the different Regiments. The flag is changed because the enemy might have a lot of our flags on hand and march upon us as friends and cut us to pieces before we discovered their designs. Hence we have an entirely different flag which will only be used by our army. We returned from picket today—had a very bad time while out. It was very cold and rained all night. So we got perfectly wet. My clothes and blankets were as wet as water. But it did me no harm that I have discovered, as I am not subject to colds. My health is remarkable good. I can stand all the exposure and hardships of camp life very well, not having been sick but once, and not that seriously since I have been in the army.

Dec 10

Dear Captain [Oscar],

I ... was very glad to hear from you and to see that you are making some progress in writing. I am sure that you can make a very smart boy if you will be particular and learn your lessons well and mind what is told you. A little boy of your age sometimes thinks that he is smarter than his parents or teachers and will not take their advice, but go his own way until he grows up, under the influence of bad and wicked companions, to be a worthless, trifling fellow that everybody will dislike.... I hope that you have good sense enough to know how to behave yourself ... to speak the truth on all occasions and never tell a story though it may seem at the time to give a great advantage. Be honest and truthful and honorable in all your dealings, [and] be kind to your brothers and sister and attentive to what is told you. I am very lonesome since Dock left me as I have to stay nearly all the time by myself in my tent. I have so many sick men in my company that I have everything to do, which keeps me very busy indeed. I have been for some weeks without a Lieutenant, Sargeant, or Corporal.... I would be very much pleased indeed to visit home and see you all. I am very anxious to see you and Billy and Charley Boy and Little Sis [Emma]. I don't think I would know her—as I have no idea how she looks, and the baby I am certain I would not know, so you and Billy will have to introduce me ... to these little folks. I hope I can be at home to see you all at Christmas, but cant promise.

Dec. 18th

I am now completing my winter residence, which I look upon as a great luxury and comfort. My residence consists of the roughest log house you ever saw, without a nail in it, without a door or window ... and a dirt floor, but rude and common as it is I assure you that I consider it a great luxury and think myself living in magnificent style.... Man's wants are but few in this life, that is his actual necessities, for I feel now that I am living in magnificent style, though while at home I would have considered it quite plain and uncomfortable. My opinion is that all new married people should commence life in just such a house as I now possess and if in the course of time they should be so fortunate as to be able to build a new house ... they could then appreciate the change & improvement.

The 23rd North Carolina Infantry remained in winter bivouac at Union Mills, Virginia. Blacknall was not granted leave to share Christmas with his family, furloughs being granted in case of sickness and "as I have the bad luck to keep well I am yet unable to get a furlough." His cheerful good humor no doubt helped his men get through the holiday season, but in his private moments he must have longed to be at his comfortable residence, surrounded by friends and family. Still dreaming of battle, the men and boys of the 23rd would face their first killing volleys at the Battle of Seven Pines five months later.

1862

The 23rd North Carolina Infantry remained at Union Mills until the early spring of 1862. The months of January and February were severe, with snow, sleet, or rain falling daily. Illnesses such as pneumonia, typhoid fever, and dysentery were rampant.

Feby 6 1862

The weather is extremely bad and the roads worse than you can imagine.... I have to ride … frequently to Manassas & I assure you that I have never seen or imagined anything like the condition of the roads & streets. I see at every turn horses dead on the road side, or buried in the mud & unable to extricate themselves, wagons without number stuck fast in the mud and deserted, together with numbers of sights which shock humanity, such as men wading nearly up to their waists in mud … all satisfying me that war in any phase is terrible.

In March Captain Blacknall traveled home for two weeks to recruit. Toward the end of March, in preparation for an advance by General George McClellan's Federal forces on the Virginia Peninsula, Confederate authorities began moving troops from the Manassas area to Yorktown. The 23rd moved by rail and steamer to Yorktown, where they were placed under the command of General D. H. Hill, who commanded the left wing of the defensive line.

April 10, 1862
Bro. George,
We are now near Yorktown…. We have suffered terribly of late, having been exposed to constant rain for four days without shelter and the weather extremely cold. Many of our boys are becoming sick from exposure but they have already borne more than I thought humanity could stand…. The enemy in very large force [is] in sight, say 300 yds. from our entrenchments. We are firing on each other constantly and the shells are bursting all around us…. The enemy's fleet is now lying in full view of us, and we landed near enough to them to be shelled by their long guns. Several of our men were shot yesterday.

April 22, 1862
Dear Jinnie:
[W]e have suffered terribly from exposure for the last four weeks, have

been most of the time without blankets or bedding of any kind, also cooking utensils, have slept on the ground without tent or cover in the worst weather I ever saw. It has rained constantly and been extremely cold. We are now lying in the trenches in the mud, and have stood a constant fire from the enemy for five days, the balls whistling around our heads…. I had a very near escape a few days since while out in front of our trenches posting the pickets. I was attacked by the enemy's sharpshooters … the bullets trimmed around me on all sides…. We have been compelled to take the enemy's fire from their batteries & gun boats for five days. I have become quite adept at bowing as I very politely *come down* when a shell bursts over me, which being so frequent I have become extremely polite.

Captain Blacknall and his men remained in the Yorktown trenches for nearly a month, often knee-deep in water. On May 5, 1862, they were ordered forward to support Confederate troops during a rear-guard assault by Federal forces at Williamsburg. Expectations for battle were high, and after advancing in double-quick time through heavy timber and across ravines, the Confederates only exchanged a volley of musket fire with Federal pickets. In a letter to Jinnie Charles mentioned "the affair is hardly worth naming" and that he was personally complimented by General Hill regarding his actions on the field. After repelling the attack, the Confederate forces moved northward to Richmond.

General Joseph Johnston, commanding the defense of Richmond, attacked the Federal army at Seven Pines on May 31, 1862. Major Blacknall and his regiment were placed in line on the

Confederate left, facing at last their long-awaited first battle with the enemy. They advanced toward the Union position at about 1:30 in the afternoon, struggling through swamp and thicket. At the edge of the felled timber and abatis a "terrific fire" was received from the enemy. Charles described the battle to his brother George shortly afterwards:

> Their batteries and riflement poured the most destructive fire into our ranks, mowing down our men by the score, our Brigade only being engaged, while others were coming to our support.... We continued to advance, slowly however as we were staggered frequently by the galling fire.... My company distinguished itself & won the praise & admiration of all who witnessed their many feats of gallantry & daring. They never quailed before the enemy, but fought on against the most desperate odds, until we were nearly all cut down.... For myself I can hardly say how I came off alive but I am still safe with four immaterial wounds, which I don't regard. I had my ankle sprained some days since & could not walk so I had to go in the action on horseback, which made the exposure much greater. I was struck with a ball in the right leg, making a slight flesh wound, another in the right foot, another on the left leg, another on the right arm, another slightly on the face. My horse was shot under me receiving four wounds with shot and shell ... & reared up and fell back dead, catching me under him and inflicting a stunning wound.... The contest waged for about two hours, and that at short range, both parties contending for the redoubts & batteries. They were alternately taken & lost, until finally we captured the whole concern, camps, tents, baggage, artillery & all, and we slept in their tents, that is those of us who were left to enjoy the victory.

Shortly after the Battle of Seven Pines, Charles Blacknall took leave and arrived unannounced by night train at Kittrell's Springs. He rode to his home the following day in George's buggy. The anxious group of family, children, and slaves at the front gate did not recognize him until he called out greetings. As his son Oscar recalled:

> Where was our father? Surely that thin, drooping man ... could not be he. Far gone from it was the erect carriage, the sparkling black eye so characteristic of our father, as well as all the pomp and circumstance of war—all the gold lace and buttons and brave plumes. The garb was plain gray without insignia or rank. The head was covered with a slouch hat of gray or drab.

When they recognized his voice, the children clambered into the wagon. Charles greeted his wife and mother with formality and reserve, and limped into the house with untied shoes. He remained before the fire the rest of the day, recounting tales of battles and marches to an attentive audience. His strength began to improve with the rest and good food of the "Springs," and he rode to the resort daily, which continued to be crowded with civilian guests and Confederate officers on leave. It was during this 30-day furlough that Captain Blacknall was promoted to major, as a result of his gallantry in battle at Seven Pines. Oscar remembered "he attached to each lapel of his coat a small solid gold star fastened with a pin." Shortly thereafter Major Blacknall returned to his regiment, which had just fought the Seven Days Battle during his absence. In a letter to his wife dated July 10, Charles wrote:

I have written to you twice since I left home & have not received a line from you or Bro Geo or heard from home at all. I hope that I did nothing or said nothing to hurt your feelings while with you, for you looked so serious when I left, but perhaps that it was owing to the fact that I was leaving home, that made you more sad than usual. This leaves me in moderate health, but not entirely well … we have been without food or water for much of the time, which went very hard with me…. I sincerely hope that the war may soon close when I can return home & live in peace & quiet with you & the children, for only in that way I can spend my time happily, but here all is turmoil & confusion, death & blood & ghastly corpses, which don't at all suit me.

In addition to the lack of food, the weather was brutally hot and dusty, which contributed to Blacknall's weakened state. Discovering that he had been nominated as a candidate for the North Carolina House of Commons with strong local support, combined with his belief that the war would be won by the end of winter, Charles considered the possibility of returning home as a state representative. After maintaining a feigned disinterest in the election results, when learning of his defeat he wrote "I was defeated only on political grounds & not personal as I can beat any man in the crowd on personal popularity. I am satisfied that I can better serve the country in the field."

As the 23rd North Carolina Infantry began preparations to march northward to join General Lee's army of Northern Virginia in late August, Major Blacknall's health further deteriorated. He was hospitalized while his regiment departed; the group would later take losses at the Battles of Fox Gap and Antietam. In early September, Charles returned home unexpectedly on sick furlough. Tired and feverish, his bedrest and recovery were constantly interrupted by visitors. At the end of his 30-day leave, Charles boarded the train to Richmond to rejoin his command. While in Richmond he shipped a trunk full of fine clothing and "confectionaries" to his family in Beech Spring. On November 7th he wrote to Jinnie that the army was marching south from Culpeper, Virginia, and that

> It is now snowing very fast & the ground covered which makes me feel uneasy about you all at home as I am fearful that you may not be well provided with wood & besides the Negroes are without shoes. I cannot get shoes or leather here at any price, so you must buy them there, regardless of price…. I imagine that our army is suffering greatly now as the men are entirely without tents & many of them without shoes or blankets.

Charles left for Gordonsville on November 27th, where he was reunited with the 23rd North Carolina Infantry on their way to Fredericksburg. The regiment occupied a defensive position at the rear of the Confederate line during the Battle of Fredericksburg, where they were subjected to heavy artillery fire. After the carnage ended

> there [was] a flag of truce for three days to bury their dead & I believe the work of interment is scarcely yet completed…. Our men went to work robbing the dead without ceremony, and many were stripped of all their clothing, presenting a strange appearance lying on the field…. [Later] I visited the Yankee lines

during the truce & conversed with their officers.

1863

The regiment spent the winter of 1862–1863 in quarters near the town of Fredericksburg. Initially the men were without tents and suffered severely from the cold weather. Opposing pickets would sit on the banks of the Rappahannock River and converse across the water. Major Blacknall spent Christmas Day on a court-martial board, and ate "a cold and very poor supper & wound up the day by retiring to bed in a cart body half filled with straw, with my shawl for covering." February brought heavy snowfall, followed by days of rain, making the roads impassable with up to six feet of mud. Major Blacknall, did however, make a trip home in the first part of the month to visit with his family. In a letter to Jinnie dated March 7, 1863, Charles wrote

> You ask my opinion of the war & the prospects of peace. I can only answer that all human calculations have proved unreliable in regard to predictions concerning its terminating. I thought & so did all persons of intelligence with whom I conversed that the prospects of peace at an early day were very good one month ago, but the Yankees have taken fresh hold, have passed the conscription act, which may prolong the war indefinitely.

Obviously concerned about her husband's health and the rigors of the upcoming campaign, Virginia Blacknall urged him to retire from the service and return home. Charles responded,

> You advise me to employ a substitute & resign my commission & come home. My answer is that while I would rejoice above all things to be at home & in peace … still as long as the war continues I intend to remain at the post of duty, let the trials & dangers be ten fold what they are. If my rations are reduced to bread alone & the suffering & exposure doubled, and substitutes get down to ten cents apiece, I shall not employ one, as long as others who are just as good as I am and whose lives are as dear and valuable to their families, continue to bear the burdens of the war. These poor fellows are now wading through the mud & water & exposed to this severe climate, with barely any shelter & but slight clothing, with scarcely half enough to eat, and at $11 per month, while I have a fine horse to ride, a good tent with a fireplace, plenty of clothing of every description, a comfortable bed & plenty to eat, though very common fare, also a servant to wait on me, and getting good wages. So you see that my condition is rather to be envied than pitied.

Springtime brought the stirring of the Union Army, now under the command of General Joseph Hooker. The main body of the army crossed the Rappahannock west of the Confederate center, in the area of the Wilderness, Virginia. Lee moved westward from the winter camps around Fredericksburg to meet the new Union threat. Jackson's corp, with the 23rd North Carolina leading the van, marched across the Federal front to descend upon their unsuspecting right flank near the crossroads of Chancellorsville. Late in the afternoon of May 2, the sun "round and red and low," the Confederates charged on the double quick and plowed through the rear of the Union line. The Federal soldiers ran in total disorder, the 23rd "chasing them like hares." Confederate losses were light, and the men obtained several hours' sleep before the fight was renewed in the morning. The 23rd North Carolina was one of the regiments that participated in Jackson's frontal charge the following daybreak. They had advanced the farthest when the Confederates began to fall back, and by trying to hold their position without flanking support, Major Blacknall and his men were soon "surrounded and captured in a redoubt of the work which they had just carried." As this struggle was going on, Lee and the rest of his army struck the Federal positions from the east, forcing Hooker's army to retreat across the Rappahonnock River.

Following his capture, Major Blacknall was held at Old Capital Prison in Washington, D.C., and was later exchanged and arrived in Petersburg on May 23, 1863. It was from Petersburg he wrote the following account of the Battle of Chancellorsville:

> Since arriving here I learn that I have been reported among the killed at the Chancellorsville battle.... I was fearful that the report would reach you that I was killed, as the last time I saw the Col ... was in the thickest of the fight & I was suddenly surrounded & cut off by a very large force. They saw our men falling all around me & the enemy right on us bayoneting our men on all sides. This was the condition of affairs when the balance of our Brigade was compelled to retreat. I, however, continued to advance driving the enemy before me until we reached their breastworks where we were entirely surrounded, when I saw that I would lose every man unless I surrendered, which I did to

> Genl. Sickles. He treated me very kindly.... I saw many officers among the Yankees that I knew & all seemed kind & friendly as if we were not at war with each other. The soldiers of the Northern army seem heartily sick of the war, but the officers & contractors seem anxious to carry it on. They have a splendid army & the most magnificent equipments of all kinds that I ever saw....
> I am yet alive, for really it seems that Providence alone could have saved my life. The enemy were at least ten to our one & were firing on us from three points at the same time. The men were falling thick around me, one ball grazed my eyebrow breaking the skin another struck me on the right leg laming me for awhile.... I have further gratification to know that I contributed some little towards the great victory we achieved as I went farther & was captured in advance of any other officer of my rank in the army at the time. The charge being led by me consisting of about four hundred men & ten or fifteen officers from different Regiments in our Division. All of the enemy's officers complimented me highly for the daring charge which we made in the face of such heavy odds. We created a great excitement in Washington & the people followed us through the streets as if we had been wild men. I made them send me through town in a fine carriage, the rest all marched. I had the gratification of riding all over the City, the Corporal who accompanied me being a very clever fellow & permitted me to use the carriage at my own discretion. We rode through the principal streets & caused much excitement among the crowd to see a "rebel officer" riding through town & making himself so much at home. The ladies & little girls overwhelmed me with oranges apples &c. insisting that I should accept many more than the vehicle could possibly hold. After finishing my pleasure ride, I reported to the Provost Martial, who assigned me to quarters at the Old Capital Prison.

The 23rd North Carolina had lost 32 men killed, 106 wounded, and 35 missing. Following the battle, the regiment returned to Fredericksburg, where Major Blacknall was reunited with his men.

Mrs. Blacknall again appealed to her husband to retire from the service and return home, with no success. On June 3rd, 1863, the 23rd North Carolina, now part of General R. S. Ewell's 2nd Corp of the Army of Northern Virginia, began to march northward, "on the tramp to parts unknown." The heat and dust of the march was oppressive, with many of the men "falling & some dieing in the road." They passed through Culpeper and the Blue Ridge Mountains, and descended into the Shenandoah Valley, which Major Blacknall wrote "far surpasses anything that I ever conceived of in beauty & fertility. The whole country as far as the eye could reach on every side is an extensive meadow & clover field." The 2nd Corp swept through Berryville and Winchester, terrifying the citizenry, routing the Federal forces and seizing their equipment and supplies. The Confederates crossed the Potomac River on June 15th and occupied the town of Williamsport, Maryland. Major Blacknall was appointed Provost Marshall, with

the authority in all instances over the persons & property being absolute. I immediately took possession of all stores, Hotels, Bar rooms, the Bank & all other species of property, put them under guard.... The stocks are very large & goods of all descriptions cheap.... Every officer or soldier in town has to have my pass before entering a store. I have to grant passes to all the Brigadier Genls. in the Div. When I took charge of the town there was a mob breaking open stores & committing every possible depreciation, the streets were crowded with hundreds of drunken men.... The citizens were shut up in their homes & frightened nearly to death. But in less than an hour I had order & quiet restored, the stores & houses guarded, & the citizens protected. Everybody is loud in praising my management, while our Genls. are perfectly satisfied with my government of the City. I took possession of the best Hotel in town for my H. Qrs. & aids, and we are living in fine style.

By June 22 Ewell had reached Greencastle, Pennsylvania, where the men rested for a few days. Major Blacknall was amazed by the beauty and prosperity of the countryside, and the army was fully resupplied in horses, cattle, and food from the local populace. Blacknall wrote

The citizens are all hostile to us, but we are quite docile as they are frightened out of their lives, & offer us everything we wish to save them from utter destruction. I have visited a good many of the trembling culprits & gave them some wholesome lectures concerning the war & invasion of our territory.

The army continued to march northward, passing through Chambersburg and Carlisle, Pennsylvania. Ewell's orders were to cross the Susquehanna River and capture the city of Harrisburg. When Lee finally realized the enemy's position, he immediately ordered his army to consolidate around Cashtown and Gettysburg. Ewell's corp was moving southwestward on the morning of July 1st when they heard the

Lieutenant George B. Bullock, 23rd North Carolina Infantry (North Carolina Division of Archives and History).

the open field, without skirmisher support. Artillery fire began to rip holes in the Confederate ranks. As the Confederates closed to within 75 paces of a low rock wall nearly 550 yards in length, a concealed force of Federal soldiers rose up and poured a deadly fire into the North Carolinians from front and flank. Staggered by the heavy loss, the men advanced a few more yards before falling to the ground and taking shelter in a shallow depression in the field. Every commissioned officer except one was shot down. Lieutenant George B. Bullock recalled at the war's end that this was the only battle "where the blood ran like a branch."[2]

sounds of battle from the growing engagement at Gettysburg. Hot and tired from the march, the North Carolina regiments of Iverson's brigade were deployed with three other brigades on the line [by Maj. Gen. R. E. Rodes], which took nearly two hours. The men of the 23rd North Carolina looked across an open field of timothy that was bordered on the far side against the wooded and rock-walled slope of Seminary Ridge, the well-protected Federal position. The attack was poorly led by Generals Rodes and Iverson, advancing unevenly across

Major Blacknall was wounded through the mouth and neck, breaking his jaw and knocking out a number of teeth. Iverson's brigade lost over a third of its fighting force during the attack, including the 23rd's loss of nearly 150 killed and wounded. Captain Vines E. Turner recalled that "when the brigade went from its position in the hollow its dead and wounded lay in a distinctly marked line of battle from one end to the other…. A member of the Twenty-third lying stone dead, his musket clinched in his hand and five bullets through his

Looking from the Federal position, a view of the field across which Blacknall and the 23rd North Carolina advanced. Blacknall fell wounded, and many of his men took shelter in the depression in the middle of the photograph (photograph by the author).

head attests the close and deadly fire under which they lay."[3] The Federals were later driven back to Cemetery Ridge, the defensive position they held at the end of the first day of fighting.

The wounded officers were transported in wagons during Lee's night retreat through the mountains after the Battle of Gettysburg. Major Blacknall "decided that he could make it on horseback and let someone worse off than he was take his place in the ambulance." The train of wagons, animals, and suffering wounded was harassed during the retreat by General Kilpatrick's Federal cavalry. A torrential rain added to the confusion of the night march over the mountain roads. Major Blacknall, worn

out from the riding and the effects of morphine, decided to rest at a roadside house until daybreak. Later that night he was captured by a Federal cavalry patrol. When he was turned over to Kilpatrick the following day, the general noticed his fine mount and swapped horses. Major Blacknall discovered a rubber coat strapped to the back of Kilpatrick's saddle, which he put on over his gray uniform. A few hours later he rode away from the Union forces unnoticed, only to be recaptured and returned to Kilpatrick by three lost Federal soldiers who were searching for their commands.

Lieutenant Wharton Green, a friend of Blacknall's from North Carolina, wrote about their reunion in the crowd of prisoners being marched to the rear that evening:

> On stopping for dinner, an old friend, Major C. C. Blacknall, came up and asked how I was off for transportation, and upon being told, he remarked: "I am pretty much in the same plight, and don't propose to stand it any longer." This was said with some difficulty of articulation, as he had had a pretty rough operation of dentistry two days before, a musket-ball entering one side of his jaw, taking out a half-dozen of his teeth, and coming out on the other. Continuing, he remarked: "I see a very neat little turnout under those trees there. Let's go and take possession"; which was done. Soon an aide-de-camp rode up and demanded to know what we were doing in General Custer's carriage. The reply came—"We are wounded prisoners, and demand the right of transportation." He went back to his commander and reported, and soon returned to us with the gratifying message: "The General says you may ride in it the rest of to-day, but he will be damned if you haven't got to look out for other accomodation to-morrow." Shortly after starting on the evening march and reaching the top of a high hill, a courier came dashing in ... and reported that Stuart was near by and then advancing. The head of the column was at once turned and we went down that hill faster than we came up, reaching the village below. Everything was in a state of confusion. Blacknall remarked to me in an undertone: "Now's our opportunity. These fellows are thoroughly *panicked*, and if old Jeb would only drop a few shells over here, they would take to their heels in hot haste. Now, let's go out and lie down on the sidewalk there and groan as hard as we can." We did, and simulated broken bones as well as could be. The Dutch ladies came around, but evinced no sympathy for our woeful condition. One of them remarked: "Served them right. I wish it had taken off their heads instead." Just then the order came to continue the march ... in double quick time until about ten o'clock at night, and a halt was called, and we went into camp.[4]

The Confederate prisoners were transported to Fort McHenry in Baltimore, Maryland, where Charles was hospitalized. He wrote his first letter to his anxious family on July 27th, 26 days after receiving his wound:

> My Dear Jinnie,
>
> I now have an opportunity of getting a line to you [and] take pleasure in saying that I am getting on very well. My wound is improving very fast, and I hope will soon be well. My jaw was broken but it is curing up without leaving any permanent injury, the scar being very small where the bullet went through my face. So my beauty will not be much impaired. I find great inconvenience in using my jaw, so I am quite a cheap boarder.... We have received the very comfortable assurance that we would all be hanged by way of retaliation but I have no hopes or fears of realizing these flattering promises, as I do not think that either Government will begin the unholy work of murdering prisoners, but on the other hand I hope to live many years among my family & friends when I can look back on all the toils and trouble endured willingly in the cause of the country as some dark dream of night from which I will awake to enjoy the sunshine of peace & prosperity.... How I wish to see you all!

Major Blacknall and other Confederate officers were sent by rail to Johnson's Island in Lake Erie around August first, 1863, less than a week after his newest child, Annie, was born. Upon arriving, he indicated it was a "very pleasant place in summer and fall, but will be very cold in winter." On September 1st he wrote to George that

> I was greatly delighted to hear from you, being the first word from home for three months, was very glad to know that you are prospering this season at the Springs. I have much anxiety & solicitude concerning you all & our affairs at home, as I hear nothing directly & everything with a gloomy aspect.... This leaves me quite well in health & spirits & getting on well.... I have many friends here. Was extremely sorry to hear of the death of Col. Christie. Write immediately & give me all the news. My best love to sister & the others of our family connections. Remember me kindly to friends generally.

Colonel D. H. Christie, commander of the 23rd North Carolina, was gravely wounded in the same attack that felled Major Blacknall during the first day at Gettysburg. He was placed in a wagon during the rough retreat through Pennsylvania, and died shortly after the Confederate army arrived at Winchester, Virginia. Major Blacknall was promoted to colonel of the 23rd North Carolina Infantry as Christie's replacement on August 15, 1863.

> September 16th, 1863
> My Dear Jinnie,
> I have just recd. your very kind & welcome letter, being the first from you.... I was rejoiced to know that all were well & prosperous about home. This leaves me very well & bearing my captivity with pious resignation, hoping however for an exchange at an early day, for I assure you that I would be rejoiced to see you & the children & Ma.... I often wander home in my dreams & see you all gathered around, but when I awake & look out at the moving, jostling, incongrous throng of prisoners,

at the broad & beautiful lake spread out before me, dotted with many sails & also at the high enclosure, where the sentinel walks his weary rounds, I am conscious that while my mind may go at pleasure my body is still at Johnstons Island.... I was pleased to know that the children are so well & progressing finely with their studies. Keep them at school as much as possible. Was glad to know that little Emma recd. her ring [prison handiwork made from a black button inlaid with the letters of her name cut from a silver coin] & was pleased. Don't think that the late arrival [the newborn Annie] will ever supplant her, glad to know that I am so fast increasing in material wealth, but I feel quite old when I count the number of responsibilities.

The prison on Johnson's Island was built by the Federal government in 1861. The 15-foot high stockade wall was made from planks and enclosed 13 barracks, or blocks, hastily constructed from green lumber. The rooms were approximately 18 feet square, designed for 10 to 15 prisoners each. The rooms were "equipped with rough bunks or shelves in tiers of three. Each bunk, for two men, has a straw tick and shoddy blankets between which the prisoners have placed clothing and newspaper for added warmth." Overall conditions during Colonel Blacknall's imprisonment were relatively favorable: food was plentiful; books and newspapers were available to read; and a kitchen and stove were available in each block. The prisoners were generally treated with respect by the commanding officers, and what few cruelties they did suffer were administered by the undisciplined "home guards" who patrolled the catwalks. A number of the Confederate officers could afford to purchase additional articles they needed from the sutler store (civilian provisioner). Many passed the time playing cards, dominoes, and chess. Baseball was a popular game played in the yard, with organized teams that drew a number of fans, fellow inmates and local citizens, as well. Between morning and evening roll calls, the prisoners were free to go anywhere within the prison grounds. Curious sightseers would sail near the island to glimpse the "Confederate rabble," and occasionally bring bands to play Union songs, which would elicit resounding requests for "Dixie" from the watching Rebels. The following excerpts from letters home were written during the period of October 10, 1863, to January 17, 1864:

October 10th, [1863]
Dear Jinnie,
The weather is yet very pleasant but we anticipate some cool breezes from the Lake during the winter if we are destined to spend it here.... There are a very large collection of our officers here, about 250 from N. C. We fare very well, have plenty of nice beef, bread, sugar & coffee issued to us, besides beans, peas, &c. We get all our extras from the Sutter ... so with a small supply of "greenbacks" we get everything that we need & live quite as comfortable as we could expect.

Oct. 28th [1864]
Dear Jinnie,
...The weather now is getting quite cold, but as I have a good supply of blankets I am well prepared for the coming winter ... have managed to keep plenty of funds on hand to pay for all extras, also to pay for cooking, washing, &c. A very small sum goes a great ways, as everything is abundant & cheap.

Nov. 4, 1863
Brother George:
...I stated in a letter to my wife that I

bore my captivity with *pious resignation*. She and Ma thought that there had been a change for the better in me. I hate to destroy so many agreeable hopes, but must say that my piety is in no wise improved and you know that I was never pre-eminent for piety, whatever other virtues I may possess. Write often. Tell Sister that I fear that the turkeys, geese, Egg-nog, etc. will suffer but little from my attacks at Christmas, but I hope for the best.

December 12, 1863
Brother George:
I had hoped to be able to spend the Christmas with you, but must forego that pleasure, for be assured that I would deem it a real pleasure to see you all again and breathe once more the free air of Heaven. For while treated here with kindness enough, I still feel that restraint incident to prison life. We spend the time principally in reading, playing chess, and discussing the topics of the day, present, past and future, much anxiety being daily felt concerning the arrival of the mail and express, and also about the approach of the meals, which is quite a consideration with us. Our buildings are large and comfortable but are becoming much crowded by recent arrivals from the West.

December 21st 1863
Brother George,
We are now having very cold weather, the lake presents one broad expanse of ice & offers fine sport for skating, which however I have not much enjoyed yet, as there is a 20 ft fence intervening.... I think very often of your ice houses when I see such an abundant supply.... Christmas is at hand & finds me still on Johnson's Island.... But when I look back over the events of the year & see the many friends by whom I was surrounded last Christmas, full of life & health & hope then, & who have since fallen, many of them had as fine promise of the future as myself & perhaps more deserving than I, when I contemplate these

things I am compelled to think that I am exceedingly fortunate in being able to say that I am not only alive, but well & doing well as I could reasonably expect.

1864

Jany 17th [1864]
Bro. George,
I am now thawed out, after being in a state of snake-like torpidity for some weeks. Imagine if you can the thermometer at 30 or 40 degrees below zero, all nature locked in an icy embrace, suppose yourself at the north pole in midwinter, a terrible gale blowing from the coldest point & you may have a faint conception of the weather we have had. But fortunately having a good supply of clothing and blankets I kept above the freezing point & am now all right. We have been greatly exercised on the subject of exchange recently, but I am yet unable to form any idea in regard to the probable time of our release.

During Major Blacknall's imprisonment, the 23rd North Carolina Regiment was involved in minor actions in the late fall of 1864, and suffered slight losses during the action at Kelly's Ford and the Mine Run campaign in Virginia. The 23rd then built winter quarters near Orange Court House and remained there until February 1864, after which they quartered the remainder of the winter at Taylorsville, Virginia. For news of the 23rd Major Blacknall corresponded with the regimental quartermaster, Captain V. E. Turner, who indicated his letter was "eagerly perused by all your friends in Camp, all begging to be remembered by you.... Old Burrows is as fat & chuffy as ever & often wonders when the Maj will return.... We all

miss you very much & hope something may turn up to let you out." The regimental surgeon, Robert I. Hicks, wrote Charles that "we are near Orange Court House & surrounded by much fine society, had a Christmas dinner of good dimensions & drinking a little champagne remembered you & the absent ones, but hope even in your confinement you had as pleasant time." And Colonel R. D. Johnston, commander of the 23rd, indicated to Major Blacknall that "in your absence the firm feel that they have lost the great manufacturer of fun & enjoyment & they refuse to be comforted."

The main activity in January at Johnson's Island was to try not to freeze to death. The weather remained unbearably cold, and wood fuel for the stoves was depleted. Prisoners huddled around the few stoves that remained burning. More than two dozen men died from exposure in January and February, and many others suffered frostbite. Despite the severe weather, a recreational, large-scale snowball fight was held in late January, "complete with military tactics, chain of command and Rebel yells ... at dark it was 'a drawn battle ... and a large number of sore heads and black eyes.'"

In early February 1864, Colonel Blacknall was transferred to Point Lookout, Maryland, to await exchange. He wrote to Jinnie on February 24:

When I last wrote I was very unwell, but said nothing about it as I did not wish to render you uneasy. I attribute my sickness to cold taken about the first of Jany. I got one of my feet slightly frostbitten, so that I was unable to wear my boots, which gave me cold, causing chills, fever,

&c. but by kind & good medical treatment here, I am again nearly all right. I am much pleased with the change of localities.... I think often of you & the children & desire greatly to see you all. I frequently walk the beach & gather beautiful collections of pebbles and shells, & I think how much pleased Emma would be if I could send her a nice assortment, I have never seen them without thinking of her.

Upon his exchange, Colonel Blacknall made his way to Taylorsville to again rejoin his command, arriving March 17. Blacknall found "my friends here jubilant at my return ... was complimented last night by a serenade from the Brigade Band, & called on for a speech." He remained in camp for a few days before traveling home to Kittrell's Springs for a seven-week period. His oldest son, Oscar, recalled:

This home coming of my father I can not remember [well]. It seems odd that I can not. I can see him reared back in one of the black, green bottomed chairs in my grand mother's room at Beech Spring telling Mr. Parrish about his battles.... Again I see him walking through the Hines place to meet my uncle ... and go to Oxford with him in a buggy, and how anxious I was that all the ... neighbors should see him in the splendid uniform he wore.... Above all I was impressed by the great change that had come over him. He looked older—like the father of the man that left rather than the man himself, and much soberer and more thoughtful. When he talked there was all that old time sprightliness but at other times he was languid, appearing tired and care worn.... The day he left [May 7] he [mounted] his sorrell and rode very close to the front porch to shake hands with me. "When are you going to come home again, Pa?" I asked. "I don't know, Captain, I may

never come any more" was his quiet answer. Then he galloped off up the road [to the Kittrell depot].

After boarding the train about 10 o'clock in the morning, Colonel Blacknall learned the railroad had been cut by Federal forces near Weldon, North Carolina. Determined to reach his regiment, he returned to Kittrell's Springs on the night train, arriving at midnight. Without awaking his family, he walked home and stirred his faithful servant Peyton, who rose and saddled his horse. They shook hands, and Peyton watched him "ride off in the dark till the shadow of the big white oaks that the road then ran under suddenly swallowed him up."

Upon reaching Petersburg, Virginia, two and a half days later and reporting for duty, Colonel Blacknall was assigned to command the northern defenses of Petersburg. He was pleased with the size of the command (several regiments, a section of artillery, and siege guns), and the fact that "there is no other officer north of the Appomattox until I reach Genl. Beauregard's command." He wrote further that

I am elegantly quartered in a magnificent mansion, surrounded by one of the finest yards & lawns I ever saw. On the balcony of the house is a large cage or small room filled with birds of all kinds canaries, &c &c. & in addition to all these beauties I had strawberries for supper, so you can see I am prospering pretty well. Two shells fired by the enemy have passed through the house, one entered the room in which I write doing no damage, but breaking some elegant furniture.

Upon learning of the 23rd's bloody fighting at Spotsylvania Court House while he was stationed in Petersburg, Major Blacknall requested to be "relieved of my present command in order that I may report for duty to my Brigade," which was granted on May 24, 1864. Blacknall finally returned to his regiment in time to direct them during the Battle of Cold Harbor:

> On the Field June 3rd [1864]
> Dear Jinny,
> I am yet well & unhurt though I have been constantly under fire for four days, we are now lying in the trenches, both sides firing incessantly the enemy making constant efforts to carry our entrenchments & being invariably repulsed…. It is impossible for them to carry our fortifications & they get their men slaughtered by hundreds in attempting it. They are now shelling us furiously. I am in command of our Brigade, Genl. Johnston being at home wounded. I do not intend that the Yankees shall see our backs, let them come in ever so large numbers, so I hope the Brigade will suffer no discredit in my hands…. I have no fears, I am as cool & collected as if at home, though all around & about me are war & death in their most terrible form.

> Battle Field June 8th [1864]
> Dear Captain
> We have been engaged in several brisk encounters with the Yankees and have whipped them every time. I have been exposed to constant firing for six or seven days, but as we are protected by our breastworks we did not get many of our men killed or wounded. I have had several narrow escapes, many men have been shot down by my side, but I am as yet untouched…. We have had a great deal of fun running the Yankees, they come nearly up to our entrenchments & when we open our cannon & muskets on them they travel back in the greatest haste. They sometimes creep up & shoot our men from behind trees. A day or two

since a Yankee slipped up in the woods & seeing me standing near the line, fired on me, but fortunately for me the ball grazed my hat & passed through a poor fellow who was standing behind me.

The armies remained in position until June 12, when Grant began to move his army to the west. General Early's corp (including the 23rd North Carolina) was mobilized to protect Lynchburg against impending Federal attack on June 17. After battling with General David Hunter's troops and driving them westward into the mountains, the Confederates caught the retreating Yankees at Liberty, where

> [we] charged the rear of their column through the streets of the town shooting them down on every side, & leaving the dead & wounded lying on the very doorsteps of houses that they were engaged in robbing…. The ladies of the town were so much rejoiced … that they ran into the streets waving their handkerchiefs & urging our men on at the peril of their lives, the shot & shell tearing through the streets.

Early turned northward up the Shenandoah Valley, passing through Staunton to Harpers Ferry. Taking on the role of tourists, the entire army took a side-trip to view the Natural Bridge, a unique rock arch:

> [We] stacked arms & gave our men time to go down & examine this great work of the Creator. It was a grand sight to see thousands of our soldiers covered with dust … beneath this grand structure examining its wonderful proportions.

Resuming the march, the men passed through Lexington, where they "marched through the cemetery & paid our respects to the grave of Gen. Jackson, the soldiers passing by with reversed arms." They drove the Federal defenders from Harpers Ferry in heavy skirmishing, during which a shell passed between Major Blacknall and his horse as he was in the act of mounting. Later that night Blacknall was one of "a few venturesome officers who galloped down [into town] that night, fired on in every moonlit stretch by the Federal guns." On July 6 Early crossed the Potomac River into Maryland and advanced on Washington, D.C. They defeated Federal troops at the Battle of Monocacy River, where the 23rd suffered heavy losses and "Colonel Blacknall was stunned for the moment by an impact of a bullet on the head, which fortunately did not penetrate" while leading a charge through a "hot enfilading fire from the line of battle." Early's men then marched 42 miles through the choking dust and heat in little more than a day and halted within three miles of Washington D.C., only to find the works too heavily defended to attempt an assault. He retreated that night, and crossed into Virginia on the morning of July 14.

The Federals began to gather in force at Harpers Ferry, their cavalry suddenly active and harassing the Confederate rear. They struck the Confederate army's wagon trains on July 16, inflicting some loss. Skirmishing continued around Berryville and Winchester.

On July 20 General Ramseur's division, including the 23rd North Carolina, was surprised by a large force of Federal cavalry at Stephenson's Depot, where the Confederates fled in disorder. Following the defeat, the *Richmond Sentinel* wrote a disparaging piece accusing

the North Carolina troops of running without firing a gun. Outraged, Colonel Blacknall immediately wrote to his brother George and indicated that his men immediately advanced towards the enemy "under a heavy and destructive fire." They were within 60 yards of the Federal line of battle when the brigade on their left began to fall back, and soon they joined the disorderly retreat. Blacknall wrote further that "[only] the Twelfth and Twenty-third North Carolina Regiments ... could be rallied.... The enemy had many killed and wounded in our immediate front, which indicated very conclusively that we were not stampeded without firing a gun as these veracious correspondents would make the readers believe." In a letter to his son Oscar dated July 31, 1864, Colonel Blacknall wrote,

> the other Brigade (there being but two in the field) suddenly gave way in confusion, which compelled us to run for dear life, this was the first time the Yankees ever saw my back in a fight, but it was run or die & of course we preferred the former.

Four days later Early's army struck the Federal forces under General George Crook at Kernstown, routing them across the Potomac and freeing Confederate officers that had been captured at Stephenson's Depot:

> [We arrived] near Winchester to find the hills & forts around town filled with Yankees, we deployed our columns, ordered a general advance & swept like an avalanche over every obstacle driving the Yankees before us & causing them to flee for their lives in every direction, leaving their dead & wounded in our hands. We felt that we were at least even with them

on the other Winchester fight [Stephenson's Depot] as their rout was most complete. In retreating ... the Yankees destroyed much of their transportations, the road for many miles was lit up by the burning of their wagons.

After chasing the Union troops into Maryland, Colonel Blacknall stopped to purchase a horse in Williamsport, where he had been the Provost Marshall the previous year on the march to Gettysburg. The citizens were delighted to see him, and

> took possession of me [and] carried me to their houses & treated me with the most distinguished kindness on account of our old acquaintance while I was with them. I have never been treated so well & met with so many kind welcomes before. These people too are nearly all Yankees.

A large Federal force under General Phil Sheridan began to gather at Harpers Ferry. The month of August was largely spent marching and countermarching, maneuvers designed to mislead Sheridan regarding Early's total strength. The Confederates, when possible, also harvested grain in the Shenandoah valley to feed their army. Again rankled by a tongue-in-cheek editorial in the Richmond paper regarding their harvesting efforts, Colonel Blacknall wrote to his family:

> You have seen, perhaps, some facetious descriptions of our doings and not doings in the Richmond *Examiner*. The descriptions are drawn in the *Examiner's* inimitable style and quite laughable withal to one at a distance. Still the "frugal swains" and the "gentle sheperds" have not had quite so gay and festive a time as one might imagine; we have, it is

true, been engaged in reaping and thrashing and gathering supplies from the teeming abundance in the country; but the piping and fiddling and feasting and frolicking, exist in the editor's fertile imagination. The lowing and bleating here are the beef cattle which affords some very tough steak and the meandering, bubbling streams and gentle flowing rivulets are often very muddy pools from which man and mules all drink indiscriminately, neither thinking themselves better than the other. If, however, any gentleman is disposed to believe that this is a gay thing, all I can say to him is, that we have a good opening for any such to come and try it.

Colonel Blacknall faithfully sent letters to his family at every opportunity, describing his adventures and inquiring of their state. He yearned for letters from his loved ones, and found their unexplainable silence confusing and hurtful. "Many, many times have I written home, but still no answer," he wrote in a letter to Virginia. "Under ordinary circumstances I should be very uneasy, but owing to our rapid & constant movements I suppose we do not get letters regularly, tho many come to others of my acquaintance. I have received no letter from home in more than two months."

Colonel Blacknall finally received letters from Jinnie and Oscar on August 28, 1864:

> Dear Jinny,
> I have just recd Oscars letter enclosing one from you which is the first line for nearly three months from home, tho, I have written many, many times. Our position here is such that it is difficult & inconvenient frequently to send letters, as we are 100 miles from the railroad. Since I last wrote, we have had a very

exciting & active campaign…. We have fared pretty hard recently, have nothing but beef & bread but on very well on that. We get plenty of apples, which is the only fruit in the valley…. I can give no opinion in regard to our future movements, we are in a days march of the river & may cross at any time…. Our men continue in fine health & spirits considering that they have marched over 1000 miles since we left Richmond, but I think I prefer marching & fighting here, to being blowed up in the trenches around Richmond. I hope to be able to get home sometime during winter if no accident occurs, in the meantime you must do the best you can.

In a letter to brother George dated September 9, 1864, Charles wrote:

We are now quietly reposing, our enemies having just been sent across the Opequon … & we being temporarily relieved from the innocent diversions of blowing out peoples brains or having our own blown out in turn, are now engaged in "our pastoral pursuits" of herding our cattle, threshing our grain & other such pastimes…. The manners & customs of this country are totally different from ours, there is a freedom, cordiality & want of reserve here, to which you are a stranger in our country & this pervades the highest as well as the middle classes, pass a house today & get a glass of water; tomorrow call & you are an old acquaintance & dear friend of the family. The poor people live in two-story brick houses & the rich, the female portion, do their own labor. I have seen many ladies of good appearance & good estate attending to their domestic affairs bare-footed & not seeming in the least confused to meet company in that seemingly uncivilized condition…. No adventures worth the mention, in fact, what you might consider an adventure of some importance has become to me only an every day occurrence, as we are so often under fire & having little affairs

with the Yankees that we don't regard a little skirmish as anything at all. At an early period of the war we were greatly excited when we knew the enemy were in the vicinity, but now I frequently lie down & read the newspapers without any concern or excitement, while my men are engaged in a brisk skirmish.

General Jubal Early, commander of the Confederate forces, had sparred with General Phil Sheridan for the past month in the Valley and concluded that he was "without enterprise, and possessed an excessive caution which amounted to timidity." Early was not aware that Sheridan had direct orders from Grant not to attack. On September 16, Sheridan learned from a Winchester spy that Early had divided his army, sending away a division and twelve guns. The following day Sheridan compelled Grant to let him attack.

Two days later a Federal reconnaissance indicated Early's remaining force of 11,400 men was sprawled across the northern and eastern approaches to Winchester, some divisions 13 miles apart. The evening of September 18 found Ramseur's division camped astride the Berryville Pike about a mile east of Winchester. General R. D. Johnston's Brigade, including Colonel Blacknall and his command, were thrown out on picket in the most forward position along the road. Opposing Federal forces were a mile further east, on the other side of Opequon Creek.

Colonel Blacknall was awakened at daybreak by the intense firing coming from the direction of his pickets near Opequon Creek. He mounted his horse and rode forward to discover Yankee cavalry crossing the creek, driving in his pickets in haste and confusion. Black-nall formed his regiment across the pike on an open plain to meet the spearhead of the Federal offensive. "A few minutes later," wrote a member of the 23rd, "an overwhelming force of cavalry, closely followed by infantry, charged our weak regiment. Disputing every inch of ground, making stand after stand, we were driven back upon the brigade and that upon the division."[5]

An observer wrote

> There was not a fence nor a house nor a bush nor a tree to obscure the view. Away off, more than two miles, we could see the crest of the hill covered with a cloud of Yankee cavalry, and in front of them (five hundred yards in front) was a thin gray line moving off in retreat solidly, and with perfect coolness and self-possession.... The scene was as plain as day. A regiment of cavalry would deploy into line, and then their bugles would sound the charge and they would swoop down on the thin gray line of North Carolinians. The instant the Yankee bugle sounded, North Carolina would halt, face to the rear rank, wait until the horses got within one hundred yards, and then fire as deliberately and coolly as if firing volleys on parade drill. The cavalry would break and scamper back, and North Carolina would "about face" and continue her march in retreat as solemnly, stubbornly, and with as much discipline and dignity as if marching in review.[6]

The 23rd faced the initial charges of the Federal cavalry (armed with new repeating Spencer carbines), and gradually fell back to the other elements of Johnston's brigade (1st, 5th, 12th, and 20th North Carolina Regiments). The spirited resistance and inspired leadership of these troops delayed the Federal

advance enough to allow Early to gather his dispersed forces and reinforce Ramseur's division.

While directing his men from horseback in the immediate rear of his line, Colonel Blacknall "received a very painful wound in his right foot ... the ball entered just below the ankle pointing downwards fracturing some of the small bones." Blacknall tried to remain in the field, but the wound was too painful and he was taken to the rear, where he "stood the whole operation (of extracting the ball) finely. The surgeons think his foot can be saved, he is doing finely as gay as can be."

As Early's forces began to withdraw through Winchester, the surgeons decided against taking Colonel Blacknall on the retreat, fearing it would worsen his condition. He was taken in by a Mrs. Smith, a local resident. As the 23rd marched by the house in the late afternoon, Blacknall waved goodbye from his open window.

Colonel Blacknall was faithfully attended by members of the community and the Federal surgeons, who recommended amputation of the injured foot. Blacknall "had scouted the idea ... when mentioned by one surgeon before the retreat, declaring that he would yet live to dance on that foot, something that distressed his pious mother greatly when she heard of it, though no one had ever known him to dance even when he had two sound feet."

As the weeks passed his condition began to worsen, and he was wracked by diarrhea. His wound continued to be quite painful, and he slept roughly under the influence of opium. Nearly a month after the Battle of Winchester

"Waverly," the residence near Clearbrook in which Colonel Blacknall was cared for, and later died (photograph by the author).

he found the strength to write a brief letter home:

October 16th [1864]
My Dear Wife,
Four weeks have elapsed since receiving my wound & yet I am lying on my back without any power to move. This is the first day that I have been able to write excepting a few days after the battle, when my foot had not become so swollen & painful. For the last 12 or 15 days I have suffered the most intense agony, all the opiates that could be administered, failed to relieve the pain or to give me any rest, for more than a week I never closed my eyes to sleep, nor had I any appetite for a particle of food. I have regreted that my foot was not amputated at first, but I trust that the worst is past & that my foot can be saved. My Surgeons think I am improving. I am greatly reduced but shall keep in good spirits. I am well cared for, so don't suffer

an uneasiness. With best love to Ma & the dear children I am yrs. afft.
C. C. Blacknall

One day a loud cannonading was heard, which roused Colonel Blacknall from his stupor. "His drowsiness disappeared, and [he] looked just like himself. He had [his servant] take him up and put on his uniform and place him by the window. He must have thought that the Confederates were advancing. As long as the firing continued his alertness held. As that died down and ceased drowsiness again possessed him." His servant undressed him and returned him to his bed.

Blacknall's condition did not improve, and his leg was finally amputated below the knee on November 6. "The amputation he bore very well," wrote

Mrs. D. B. Smith, in whose home he rested, "but he was afflicted with the worst form of Dyspepsia, indeed his digestive organs seemed to have given way completely, he lost his appetite, & in no way could we restore it. He suffered so much from [diarrhea] and debility that it was only occasionally he liked to have anyone in his chamber."

His servant, Hundley, was constantly at his side, and he was frequently visited by Mrs. Smith and her sisters. Dr. Lawson, the attending surgeon, finally told Colonel Blacknall his condition was very grave. "He bore the announcement better than Dr. Lawson supposed, & when we asked him if he would like to see a clergyman he said 'yes send for one, & send quickly' … in the meantime he was so anxious that some one should pray for him that I did so myself."

The Blacknall family waited anxiously for news of Charles. They had heard conflicting rumors of his health—that he was dead, that he was walking about Winchester on crutches, followed by "contradictions, and then by repetitions." In mid-December George Blacknall received the following letter:

Winchester, Va.
November 17th 1864
Dr. G. W. Blacknall,
Dear Sir:
It is my painful duty to announce to you the death of your Brother Col Chas Blacknall. At one time I had high hopes of his recovery but his health gave way under the severe and excruciating pain of his wound and he sunk under his sufferings, he received every attention that could possibly have been given him by the family of the house where he was taken, and I was with him 5 or 6 hours each day for ten days before his death. He received a decent burial and I have in my possession his watch, money & personal effects which shall be delivered as soon as I reach the Confederacy. In his death his family have lost an affectionate kinsman and the Confederacy a noble & gallant soldier. The family have my sincere sympathy and commiseration in this great bereavement.
Very truly yrs
John W. Lawson Surg

Colonel Charles C. Blacknall was buried in a corner of the Episcopal Churchyard in Winchester, beside the grave of Colonel Christie, the former leader of the 23rd North Carolina Infantry. Residents of Winchester, including a number of Union officers, contributed toward his burial expenses. He was later removed with the other North Carolina dead to the Stonewall Cemetery in Winchester.

The 23rd North Carolina Infantry fought on without Colonel Blacknall, and were engaged at the Battles of Cedar Creek, Hatcher's Run, and Fort Stedman. Bitter fighting followed in the spring of 1865 at Petersburg, Sayler's Creek, and Farmville, Virginia, where the regiment performed courageously and repulsed a number of Federal assaults, allowing the ragged Confederate army to continue its retreat. The regiment surrendered to Union forces on April 12, 1865, and 86 surviving members were paroled.

Postscript

Mr. Ben Ritter, a local historian and archivist in Winchester, was of great

The grave of Colonel Charles C. Blacknall, Stonewall Cemetery, Winchester, Virginia (courtesy Ben Ritter).

assistance in locating the home in which Colonel Blacknall died. While conducting research on my behalf he discovered several newspaper accounts of hauntings at Waverly in the late 19th century. Incidents included an overnight guest seeing a man dressed in a Confederate officer's uniform walk across the bedroom to the window and gaze outside. Another time several men were playing cards late at night by candlelight in the room when this same officer entered and blew out the candles. This "ghost" was glimpsed other times, as well.

Interestingly, these accounts seemed to fit Blacknall's personality. Blacknall frequently looked out the window, and near the time of his death had his servant dress him in his uniform and help him to the window. Blacknall did not approve of liquor and may have opposed gambling and card-playing; a typical Blacknall response would have been to put out the candles (this aggressive response is similar to that of Blacknall's throwing his son Oscar in the snowbank, or another incident mentioned in the Blacknall papers in which Blacknall struck a man over the head with a ledger because he had accused him of dishonesty).

What most excited me about these accounts is that the identity of this apparition was unknown. Considering that Blacknall died in the house, the ghost wore a Confederate officer's uniform, and the ghost's behavior was similar to Blacknall's, I thought that perhaps this was his restless spirit.

I had to find Waverly.

Ken and Tricia Stiles, the owners of this elegant home at Clearbrook, are some of the most gracious and friendly people I have ever met. In addition to giving me an excellent tour of the Winchester battlefields, they allowed me to spend the night in the room in which Blacknall died. I stayed up very late rereading Blacknall's letters, hoping to catch a glimpse of his ghost. The wind and rain shrieked outside (as in all good ghost stories), but I finally fell asleep, disappointed at the lack of any supernatural moments. Yet I also found comfort in the fact that if indeed this ghost was Blacknall, he had reconciled his death and was at peace, and no longer walked the hallways of Waverly.

III

An Eye for an Eye:
An Episode from
Missouri's Civil War

Introduction

This story about the Civil War in southeastern Missouri is a far-ranging piece that illustrates the conflict through the experiences of a variety of participants. Although not a major theater of the war, the southeastern counties were a violent place where very few escaped its harsh effects. Settled largely by Southerners, Missouri's decision to remain in the Union as a slave state created bitter divisions within her borders.

Missouri's allegiance and resources were coveted by the Confederacy throughout the war. The southern portion of the state was strongly supportive of the new Rebel government, and the Federal forces had the difficult task of

trying to suppress this region. Bands of guerrillas murdered and plundered at will, often in the name of the Confederacy. Severe measures by Union authorities, including the seizure or destruction of property owned by Southern sympathizers, led to widespread hatred and more retaliatory violence. The mistrust and small-scale warfare continued to escalate during the war. The wartime courtesies that routinely occurred between opponents in the eastern theater were scarce in Missouri's bloody southeastern counties, where this story took place.

The core of this history is the telling of two related stories at the same time. The first is that of six Confederate soldiers who were members of General Sterling Price's Confederate army, which marched into Missouri in the fall of 1864. These men—Asa Ladd, Harvey Blackburn, George Bunch, James Gates, John Nichols, and Charles Minniken— were regular soldiers captured during Price's campaign. Shortly after they arrived in St. Louis as prisoners of war, they were informed they were to be executed in retaliation for the murder of Major James Wilson and six of his men, an act they did not commit. The details of their harrowing situation are documented through a profile of Private Asa Ladd, whose prison letters to his family still exist.

Interspersed with the Ladd drama is the second story about Major James Wilson and Colonel Timothy Reves. Colonel Reves and his "independent" 15th Missouri Cavalry (CSA) inhabited the swamps of southeastern Missouri and tried to defend the area from Federal incursions. Federal authorities regarded him as an undisciplined outlaw and murderer who terrorized the Unionists in his sector. The pro-Rebel populace viewed Reves as a dedicated, if not somewhat overzealous, Confederate officer whose company of local soldiers was committed to protecting their homes and communities. Major Wilson commanded Union troops in the same area, and he and his officers were equally harsh and resolute in dealing with Reves's "guerrillas" and the citizens who supported them. Wilson and Reves had a series of minor clashes until Wilson's capture at the Battle of Pilot Knob in 1864. This second story details the development of the adversarial relationship that culminated in Major Wilson's murder as a prisoner of war by the order of Colonel Timothy Reves.

St. Louis

October 29, 1864
St. Louis, Mo.
Dear Wife and Children,
    I take my pen up with a trembling hand to inform you that I have to be shot between the hours of two and four o'clock this evening. I have but four hours to remain in this unfriendly world. There is six of us sentenced to die in the room of six Union soldiers that was shot by Reves' men. My dear wife, don't grieve after me. I am going to rest. I want you to meet me in Heaven. I want you to teach the children piety, so that they may meet me at the right hand of God. Amy, when I left home, I did not think that I would be shot under sentence, but I am in the hands of men who have the power to execute the sentence, therefore I shall submit myself into the hands of God Almighty....
    I don't want you to let this bear on your mind more than you can help, for you are now left to take care of my dear children. Tell them to remember their father. I want you to go back to the old place and try to support yourself and the children.... If you don't get this letter before St. Francis River gets up, you had better stay there until you make another crop, and you can then go in the dry season.
    It is now half past one and I must bring my letter to a close.
    Leaving you in the hand of God, I send you my best love and respects in the hour of my death. Kiss all the children for me. You need not have uneasiness as to my future state for my Faith is well founded and I fear no evil. God is my refuge and hiding place.
    Good by, Amy[1]

The second of eight children, Asa Valentine Ladd was born to Ransom and Anna Ladd of Wayne County, Missouri, on November 23, 1829. Asa married Amy Gaines in 1849 and they raised seven children on their farm in nearby Stoddard County. When war became imminent, Asa enlisted in the Confederate Army on March 10, 1861, and served with the Fourth Missouri Cavalry. Asa saw action in a number of skirmishes for the next three years. When the Army of Missouri, commanded by Major General Sterling Price, entered Missouri from Arkansas in September of 1864 to begin "Price's Raid," the Fourth Missouri Cavalry was assigned to Major General John S. Marmaduke's brigade. After Price's forces were defeated at the Battle of Pilot Knob and turned west along the Missouri River, Asa Ladd was captured by Union troops near Sedalia on October 15, 1864.[2, 3]

Southeast Missouri's Early War Years

Although the Battle of Pilot Knob was the only major action fought there during the Civil War, southeastern Missouri was one of the most war-torn areas in the United States. The division between the Union and Confederate factions of the populace was bitter and often violent. The counties of southeastern Missouri, commonly known as "Secech Country," were strongly pro-Rebel in sentiment and harbored a number of guerrilla groups of various indistinction. Loosely organized and even less disciplined, these raiders plundered and killed Union citizenry and harassed Federal scouting patrols. Richard Hudson, a Unionist, reported to General

W. S. Rosecrans, commander of the Union forces in Missouri, that

> hearing also that you had been misinformed concerning the condition of the border of the State, including Oregon, Ripley, Carter and Butler Counties, being that I am a citizen of Ripley County, I now take the liberty ... to let you know our desperate condition. There ranges in these counties above named bands of robbers ... that have ... concentrated on the line, which numbers from 600 to 1,000 men, which consists of the notorious Reves, Freeman, Reed, Boze, Barnes, and others. These bands range between our posts, Patterson, Mo., and Batesville, Ark., which is near 150 miles between. The barbarous and insufferable treatment the Union men and families get from these bands, at their discretion, the records of history hardly has a parallel. The Union men are hunted, and if found are shot or killed in some other way, and often our families are shamefully and grossly insulted by these desperate bloody-handed bushwhackers. Nor is this the worst. We not having the liberty to make a crop last year, and our property and provisions being taken away from us by those bands, there are many families without relief who shortly will be reduced to starvation ... scouting through that country will never civilize it. There has been scouting through there that has killed and captured a great many of them, but as soon as our scouts turn back, they come out of the brush and return to their former depredations.[4]

Named by Hudson and branded a "murderous fiend," a "blood-stained outlaw," and the grudgingly respectful "Old Tim" by Federal forces in southeastern Missouri, Timothy Reves was the major resistance to Union authority along the Missouri/Arkansas border. Reves was born in North Carolina on April 28,

Southeastern Missouri during the Civil War (author's collection).

1821, and moved to Ripley County, Missouri, in 1842. A Baptist preacher, Reves settled on a farm near Flat Creek, a few miles northeast of the town of Doniphan. Reves joined the Confederate service in the summer of 1861 as a captain in the Missouri State Guard, commanded by Major General Sterling Price. Reves and his men were briefly attached to General Earl Van Dorn's forces of the Trans-Mississippi Department in the spring of 1862, where they were chiefly employed as scouts. Reves left in June of 1862 and returned to Ripley County to recruit for the Confederacy and raise a company of men to scout enemy troop movements and defend the area against Union occupation.[5] Many of his men came from Doniphan and Ripley County and neighboring northeastern Arkansas. Reves and his Independent Company of Missouri Scouts ranged the wooded hills, swamps, and bottomlands as far south as Batesville, Arkansas. On July 20, 1862, Reves's men, two to four hundred strong, attacked and routed two companies of Missouri State Militia Cavalry under the command of Captain William T. Leeper at Greenville, Missouri. This raid was Reves's first military action against Federal forces in southeastern Missouri, and succeeded in outfitting his command with rifles and horses left behind by the fleeing Federals.[6]

Union opposition to the Rebel guerrillas and bushwhackers in the area consisted of small, inexperienced commands occupying widely-spaced forts at such places as Pilot Knob (Fort Davidson), Bloomfield, and Patterson. The tasks of scouting the counties, chasing bushwhackers, and breaking up recruiting operations fell largely to the 3rd Missouri State Militia (MSM) Cavalry, commanded by Major James S. Wilson. Wilson was born in Maryland on May 3, 1834, and moved with his family to Missouri in 1856, settling on a farm in Lincoln County. Leaving a family loyal to the Southern cause, Wilson enlisted as a private in Company G, 3rd MSM Cavalry.[7,8] Rapidly advancing through the ranks of First Sergeant and Captain, Wilson was promoted to Major of the 3rd MSM Cavalry in 1863, and commanded the 3rd Subdistrict of St. Louis at Pilot Knob in 1864.[9]

As indicated by many reports filed by returning Federal patrols, the guerrilla bands rarely fought as a unit when surprised and attacked, and would quickly scatter into the woods. "The countryside," wrote Captain William T. Leeper of the 3rd MSM, "is diversified by hills, valleys, swamps, marshes, generally heavy timber, underbrush, &c., interspersed with numerous creeks, rivers, and rivulets, offering all the advantages that could be desired by a guerrilla force, where they can operate, and in many places elude capture or almost defy pursuit."[10] The back roads swarmed with guerrillas and robbers, often dressed in blue cavalry coats. The Federal troops had a general policy of executing suspected guerrillas, which was variously enforced by the officers leading the scouts and patrols. This policy created an intense hatred in the local populace for any Federal authority.

The Union troops regarded the pro–Rebel citizenry as hostile and dealt with them harshly, knowing many of them supported and concealed guerrillas. Brigadier General Clinton B. Fiske, who commanded the forces in the District of Southeastern Missouri in 1863, reported that

> the fiends [guerrillas] murder none but radical Union men, while conservatives of undoubted loyalty are spared in property and person. The radicals are hunted from their homes, and their substance appropriated and destroyed. Our troops being chiefly from the radical portion of the community, it is with great difficulty that they are restrained from depredations upon the class favored by the bushwhackers.[11]

Union marauding occurred, and many homes and buildings were burned

Major James S. Wilson, 3rd Missouri State Militia Cavalry (courtesy Patsy Creech).

that were suspected to be "rebel."[12] Captain Leeper wrote that "many men and women who are at home do us more damage than the regular soldier; they feed, harbor, and conceal the guerrillas."[13]

After completing a scout through Oregon and Ripley Counties in November, 1863, Captain Robert McElroy of the 3rd MSM reported "the women in that region are even more daring and treacherous, and, in fact, worse than the men, as we found in their possession a number of newly made Rebel uniforms."[14]

General Fiske, obviously frustrated at the lack of success in containing Reves, commanded Captain Leeper to

> summon the wives of all the bushwhackers you can reach to come to Doniphan, and give them plainly to understand that either their husbands must come in and surrender themselves voluntarily and stop their villainous conduct, or their houses, stock, &c., will be given to the flames, and the families all sent down the Mississippi River, to be imprisoned.[15]

Federal soldiers were not welcome in the southeastern counties, and they found it impossible to adequately protect the unionists in the area. Federal patrols were in enemy territory as soon as they left their outposts. The troopers were often bushwhacked, and could kill only a few of the enemy before the guerrillas dispersed. Guerrilla bands continued to torment Unionist families, and supplied themselves with stolen property, or food and horses accepted from Confederate sympathizers. A resident remembered

> [one] morning ... several men came riding up and asked me what I had in the barn. I told them cows. They said, "Got any horses?" and I said, "No—yes, there is an old horse in there but he has a bad leg and won't do you any good." So they ... went in and got him—the last of our horses. They had hardly gone when a big, grizzly-bearded man came to the kitchen and ordered Ma to get him some breakfast, and while he was eating, he made his boast that the buzzards would have one Yankee to feast on.... That was "Old Tim Reves."[16]

Toward the end of the war, the incessant warfare between Union troops and "irregular" Confederate units, guerrillas, and bushwhackers took its greatest toll on the civilian population. Lawlessness was rampant. Numerous citizens had been killed, crops taken or destroyed, horses and livestock seized, homes ransacked and burned. Starvation was a reality for many families by the spring of 1865.

Asa Ladd's Imprisonment

After his capture at Sedalia, Asa Ladd was held in Jefferson City for eight days before he and other Confederate prisoners were loaded on train cars and sent to St. Louis. Asa arrived at Gratiot Street Prison in St. Louis on October 25, 1864.[17]

Captain Timothy Reves, CSA

More accurately considered a Confederate irregular or independent than a "notorious guerrilla," Timothy Reves was associated with the Confederate military in an official capacity throughout the war. After leaving the Confederate Army to raise his Independent Company of Missouri Scouts, Reves recruited in the Ripley County area, reporting Federal activities to his superiors and skirmishing with Federal patrols. "Reves' men are now infesting the country lying between Doniphan, Greenville, and Martinsburg," reported a Federal officer in March, 1863. "[They] are principally involved in enforcing the conscription law ... [and] are all dressed

A postwar image of Captain William T. Leeper, 3rd Missouri State Militia Cavalry (author's collection).

Colonel John Burbridge of the 4th Missouri Cavalry dated May 31, 1863, Reves described a skirmish with a Federal patrol in which "we never got a scratch ... our men acted bravely and orderly. We enjoyed ourselves fine except the circumstance of Captain Roberts' men at Pocahontas who became intoxicated and could not be controlled."[20] A few weeks later Reves wrote to General Marmaduke that

Everything appears quiet here at present.... It is rumored here that there was five or six thousand went from Ironton to reinforce at Vixburg. The certainty of this report I have not as yet been able to ascertain.... There is still jayhawking & stealing going on, some calling themselves Gen. Marmaduke's men, some claimed to be Reves, & some claim to belong to other commands. I think we will be able to put a stop to it in a great measure soon. Yesterday I sent out five scouts, of ten men each, for the purpose of making a grab on the jayhawkers and disserters.[21]

in Federal cavalry coats."[18] Captain Reves's command acted as a scouting advance in preparation for Brigadier General John S. Marmaduke's raid through southeastern Missouri the following month, an attempt to draw Federal troops from beleaguered Vicksburg. They later participated in the raid, which attacked Federal outposts at Bloomfield, Patterson, and Cape Girardeau.[19] Afterwards Reves returned to his activities in Ripley County. In a letter to

From his camp on Cherokee Bay, an area of dense swamp and lowland along the Black River in southeastern Missouri and northeastern Arkansas, Captain Reves wrote Marmaduke on June 13, 1863, that he had established a line of couriers from his camp to Poca-hontas and that "there are several appli-cations by Missourians to become mem-bers of my command. My company being full, I cannot take them without permission to raise another company." Reves also wanted to inform General Price that "distilleries on the borders of Arkansas and Missouri are consuming all the corn through this country ... tak-ing the forage from our horses, and leav-ing the soldiers' families in a state of suffering.[22]

Later in the summer Reves's com-mand was temporarily attached to Colonel S. G. Kitchen's 7th Missouri Cavalry.[23] According to their rolls, Reves was "sent to Southeast Mo. to re-cruit on Sept. 14, 1863." Reves's activi-ties were becoming increasingly bother-some to the Federal authority in the area. On October 27, 1863, General Clinton B. Fiske ordered Captain Leeper and 150 men to Doniphan to "give old Tim and his rascally gang such a hunt and extermination as they never yet had."[24] Leeper boasted he could do it with one hundred men, and that "now would be a fine time to be after him. The leaves are gone, and they will have to find their holes."[25] On October 31, 1863, a force of 195 Federal cavalry under the command of Leeper and Major Jose-phus Robbins (2nd MSM) caught up with Reves along the Black River in Arkansas. "The advance came up with him near night, and gave chase, press-ing him so closely that he dropped his blankets, coats, and hats, and drove him

into the swamps, his native resort."[26] Reves regrouped his men, and was re-ported to be in Butler County, Missouri, "killing some more Union men."[27] Reves continued to elude the Federal forces under the command of Major Wilson and Captain Leeper until Christmas Day, 1863, when Wilson surrounded Reves's camp and attacked by surprise, killing 35 of Reves's men and sending the rest fleeing into the woods.[28] Cap-tain Reves survived the attack, and spent a relatively quiet winter recruiting and rebuilding his company. He resumed his scouting and skirmishing activities in March of 1864, the 3rd MSM Cavalry still intent on his capture or death. Leeper wrote that "those who feed and conceal them [guerrillas] are as mean as they are, and I will kill them if the thing does not stop. If Union men are robbed, I will take their property to pay for it. If they kill a loyal man, I will kill 5 of them. I believe by this course it can be stopped."[29]*

Captain Reves was promoted to Major in the spring of 1864, and his command designated Company A, 15th Missouri Cavalry. On June 7, 1864, Reves was ordered by Brigadier General J. O. Shelby to "get your command col-lected as soon as possible and join me. Increase your command as much as pos-sible. Place every man in the service from sixteen to fifty ... should any refuse resort to any means you deem best to enforce the order.... I feel satisfied that we will be allowed to penetrate Missouri as far as we may desire."[31] Shortly

*According to Mrs. Washington Harris, a Ripley County resident during the war, "Leeper was a preacher and Tim Reves was a preacher. I guess that is the reason they was both so mean.... Nobody had much to eat and when old man Leeper came he always tried to find the stock and grain to take and the Yankee army always had plenty to eat without it needed to steal."[30]

James Madison Kitchen (courtesy Doris Riewald).

were being made for General Sterling Price's invasion of Missouri, and all available fighting men were being gathered. Promoted again to Colonel, Timothy Reves and Colonel McCray reported with their newly organized troops to Major General James Fagan at Pocahontas, Arkansas, on September 16, 1864.[33] Price's "Raid" was going to begin in three days.

St. Louis

Word first reached the Union generals in St. Louis about the apparent murder of Major Wilson and six of his men from returning Federal prisoners who had been paroled by Price on October 3, 1864. Witnesses described how Wilson and his men were singled out from the crowd of prisoners and marched away under guard, waiting for Colonel Reves's command to "come up."[34] Major General Rosecrans immediately ordered a "major and six enlisted men of the rebel army to be kept in solitary confinement until the fate of Major Wilson and his men is known. These men will receive the same treatment Major Wilson and his men received."[35]

afterwards, Major Reves and his men reported to Colonel Thomas H. McCray at Jacksonport, Arkansas. Citizens fleeing Reves's aggressive conscription efforts confirmed Federal suspicions that the Confederates were planning a major campaign. Federal scouting reports in July and August indicated Reves's strength in various camps in northeastern Arkansas at between 2,000 and 3,000 men, many of them new recruits.[32] Plans

Federal troops searched the area with no success. Then on October 23 a youth hunting persimmons in the woods found seven human bodies along St. Johns Creek. "We went out to where the bodies were with lanterns for by that time it was one hour gone into the night," wrote James M. Kitchen, a local resident. "One of the bodies we saw had on officer's clothes. The straps were those of a Major, yellow with a leaf."[36] The dead were identified as Major Wilson and his men. Wilson had been shot twice through the left breast and once in the head. Three of the other bodies "had no clothes on save their shirts and drawers ... and were so eaten by hogs that we could not distinguish a feature."[37] The remains were wrapped and brought to St. Louis in a wagon for burial. Brigadier General Thomas Ewing mourned the loss of Wilson:

> He was an officer of rare intelligence, zeal, courage and judgment, and his soldierly virtues were adorned by a purity, unselfishness and integrity of character which won him the love, respect and trust, alike of his subordinates and superiors. When the war broke out, he entered the service a private, and by that act of devotion to the Government severed almost all ties that bound him to family and home.[38]

General Rosecrans, infuriated by the murder of Wilson, wasted little time in carrying out his retaliatory threat. Rosecrans issued Special Order 279 on October 28:

> It appearing from the most conclusive evidence that Maj. James Wilson, Third Cavalry Missouri State Militia, and six men of his command, taken prisoners of war by the enemy ... at Pilot Knob, Mo., were turned over ... to the guerrilla Tim Reves, at a place near the town of

Union, in Franklin County, Mo., and that [were] subsequently brutally murdered by this blood-stained outlaw; therefore ... the following six of the enlisted men of the rebel army—James W. Gates, Company H, Third Missouri Cavalry, C. S. Army; John N. Ferguson, Company A, Crabtree's cavalry, C. S. Army; Harvey H. Blackburn, Company A, Coleman's cavalry, C. S. Army; John Nichols, Company G, Second Missouri Cavalry, C. S. Army; Charles W. Minneken, Company A, Crabtree's (Arkansas) Cavalry, C. S. Army; Asa V. Ladd, Company A, Burbridge's (Missouri) Cavalry, C. S. Army—will be shot to death with musketry within the limits of the city of St. Louis, Mo., on Saturday, the 29th day of October, 1864, between the hours of 2 and 4 p.m.[39]

Price's 1864 Missouri Campaign

The "invasion" of Missouri in 1864 by Confederate forces under the command of General Sterling Price was an act of desperation. The plan was conceived by General E. Kirby Smith, commander of the Trans-Missouri Department, and intended to create enough of a threat to draw Union troops from Lee's outnumbered forces in Virginia. The Order of American Knights (OAK), a secret pro-Confederate citizen's organization, had been recruiting all spring and summer in southeastern Missouri, and reportedly had large numbers of men ready to join Price's army.[40] The goal was a large one: invade Missouri and occupy St. Louis, thereby severing a vital transportation and communication center for the Union and seizing the Federal arsenal there to arm the

Major General Sterling Price (U.S. Army Military History Institute).

Confederate troops, and to incite the support of the pro-Rebel populace and gain thousands of new recruits.

Confederate troops for the invasion were organized that summer in Louisiana and Arkansas. Quality Confederate manpower was scarce, and the army was desperate for men. Of the 12,000 troops assembled for the raid, "about 5,000 ... were the usual character of the Confederate cavalry. The remainder were deserters and conscripts, officered by men of their own kind, to a certain extent."[41] General Sterling Price was selected to command the army, with three divisions under Generals Marmaduke, Fagan, and Shelby. "On the 19th of September," wrote Price, "I entered Missouri with nearly 12,000 men, of whom 8,000 were armed, and fourteen pieces of artillery."[42] Price marched in three columns on a wide front to confuse the enemy and make foraging easier for his army.

General Thomas Ewing, Jr., commander of the Union forces in the District of St. Louis, was aware of Price's activities but uncertain as to the location of the Confederate army. Upon his order, Major James Wilson, commander of the Third Subdistrict at Pilot knob, sent out 86 men from the 3rd MSM under Lieutenant Erich Pape to locate the Rebel advance.[43] The troopers entered the town of Doniphan at five o'clock in the morning on September 19, 1864, and encountered a small group of Confederates from Shelby's brigade. After routing the Confederates and chasing them beyond the Arkansas border, Pape and his men returned to Doniphan and burned the entire town to the ground.[44] The Federals then rode casually northwards toward Patterson, burning more homes along their route. Mrs. Washington Harris remembered they "burnt old Miss Gilasky's home and left her children sick on the ground."[45] (The following day Shelby's men reported passing "several houses burnt; women and children around the smoking ashes."[46]) Apparently not fearing retaliation, Pape's men rode until sunset and camped on the Vandiver Farm, about ten miles northeast of Doniphan, for the night. When Shelby reached Doniphan later in the afternoon, he was

shocked to find the enemy had burned the "helpless and ill-fated town."[47] That night Shelby "dispatched 150 men under Lieutenant Colonel [Rector] Johnson to pursue the vandals. They came upon them early the next morning [September 20], attacked, scattered, and killed many of them."[48] Thus the actions at Doniphan and Vandiver Farm were the first of Price's campaign.

The three Confederate columns rejoined at Fredericktown, about 75 miles north of Doniphan, on September 24 and 25, after encountering only minor resistance. They had attacked the small Federal garrisons at Patterson, Bloomfield, and Jackson and driven the Federal forces in retreat toward Pilot Knob. The towns the Confederates marched through were largely abandoned— Greenville had been deserted with "only two families in the place."[49] When the troops entered Fredericktown one soldier noted the "citizens [are] generally Southern in sentiment, many coming to greet us; recruiting."[50] Shelby's cavalry rode ahead toward Farmington, wrecking railroads and burning bridges. On September 26, 1864, Fagan's division seized the town of Arcadia. The outnumbered Union forces fell back the following day and "took refuge behind their fortifications at Pilot Knob."[51]

Asa Ladd in Gratiot Street Prison

How the six Confederate prisoners were selected for retaliatory execution is not documented. All of them were members of Price's army that arrived at Gratiot Street Prison after October 20,

1864. The prison was overcrowded with Rebel prisoners, yet all six scheduled to die were among those from Price's army to most recently arrive. General Rosecrans may have reasoned that these trainloads of Rebel soldiers were closest to the crimes committed against Major Wilson and his men. The six Confederates had filled out detailed statements[52] on October 28, in which they supplied information about their families and occupations, whether they had ever taken the Oath of Allegiance to the United States, borne arms, fought in any battles or skirmishes, or stolen property. They were also asked if they were Southern sympathizers and if they "sincerely desire to have the Southern people put down in this war?," to which they all answered "no." According to the Ladd family history, "only those prisoners who refused to take the oath of Allegiance ... were marched into a room where they were ordered to draw lots. A container which held marbles, of which there were six black ones, was held above eye level so the men could not see the color they were drawing.... Those drawing a black one were to be executed."[53] Later that day General Rosecrans issued Special Order 279, naming the six doomed prisoners. No Rebel majors were imprisoned at the time, and the first captured major would be shot in retaliation for the death of Major Wilson.

An interesting case is that of John N. Ferguson, a 23-year-old private from the 46th Arkansas Cavalry, and one of those scheduled to die. In his statement, Ferguson swore he had never taken the Oath of Allegiance and had never participated in any battles or skirmishes, having been in the hospital a great deal

and on duty as a teamster."[54] Yet a curious testament from Harvey H. Blackburn indicated that following his capture Ferguson "had taken the Oath of Allegiance to the U.S. and had joined the Federal Service at Batesville, Ark.— he did not say when this was done, but said he had done it."[55] This statement may have been an effort by Blackburn to spare Ferguson's life. Private Ferguson's case was reviewed, and the following morning Private George F. Bunch, Company B, 3rd Missouri Cavalry, was substituted for Ferguson on the execution list, "it appearing from this man's examination that he never bore arms and was only employed as a teamster."[56]

According to the *St. Louis Democrat*,[57] "the six men in Gratiot Street Prison were not informed of the doom awaiting them until the day of execution. They were greatly affected when told they were to be taken out and shot. Father Ward, of the Catholic Church, and Rev. Phillip McKim, of the Episcopal Church, visited the men in prison.... Mr. McKim baptized five of them on Saturday morning. The sixth (Asa V. Ladd) had already been baptized, and was a member of the Methodist Church."

In addition to writing to his wife Amy, Asa Ladd wrote a short letter to his father that morning of October 29:

> My Dear Father
> I am condemned to be shot today between the hours of two & four o'clock P.M. in retaliation for some men shot by Reves (Major Wilson and six men). I am an innocent man and it is hard to die for another's sins. You can imagine my feelings when I think of you, my wife, & children. I want my family to come back to my old place. If you live till peace is

Reverend Phillip McKim (courtesy Norfolk Church).

made I want you to settle up and pay off all my debts…. God is my refuge and hiding place. Meet me in Heaven. Good bye.[58]

Price's Advance

The only resistance to General Fagan's advance on Arcadia on September 26 was the determined skirmishing of Major Wilson's 3rd MSM Cavalry and attached elements of the 47th Missouri and 14th Iowa Infantry, a total force of nearly 400 men. Late in the afternoon Wilson was wounded in the forehead during a cavalry charge and fell from his horse, blood streaming down his face. He remounted and directed his men in a steady retreat until sunset, when they dug in on a ridge north of Arcadia.[59] In the darkness from the ridgeline the Federal troopers could see hundreds of Rebel campfires and listened to Price's army filling the valley below them. "It was raining a good deal," wrote Captain Charles Hills, an officer from General Ewing's staff who rode forward to Wilson's position at ten o'clock that night, "and the opposing pickets joked back and forth. We ascertained they were forming a very extensive line."[60] Hills reported back to General Ewing, who had come down from St. Louis that day and established headquarters at Fort Davidson. Ewing ordered a retreat, and at midnight Wilson's men fell back to Ironton, two miles south of Fort Davidson.

The morning of September 27 was "raining and foggy. When daylight broke … we soon saw the Rebels forming in line," reported Hills.[61] That line proved to be the 1800 cavalrymen of Brigadier General William L. Cabell's Arkansas Brigade. Scattered musket fire built to a continuous roll, and after a brief stand, the Federal pickets mounted their horses and galloped away toward Ironton, the Confederates in pursuit. As his men came in Wilson realized he was vastly outnumbered and that the only place to make a defensive stand was Ironton Gap, a narrow opening between Shepherd Mountain and Pilot Mountain, one mile to the rear. The main road to Fort Davidson and Pilot Knob passed through Ironton Gap, with the fort nestled on the plain between the two rugged hills. Wilson immediately sent his infantry, nearly 200 men, on the double-quick to defend the passage. He covered their retreat with his 200 dismounted troopers, who fired continuously at the cautious Rebel advance as they retreated steadily northward to Ironton Gap.[62]

When Major Wilson arrived at Ironton Gap at about ten o'clock in the morning, he ordered the infantry to form a skirmish line in the woods along the southern flank of Shepherd Mountain. Wilson deployed his men in the heavy timber at the base of Pilot Mountain. Thus the men were afforded maximum cover behind rocks and trees, and the artillery at Fort Davidson could contend with any direct Rebel advance through Ironton Gap. Wilson's men were dismounted with every fourth man holding horses. Shelling from the Confederate cannon and frontal attacks by regiments of Cabell's cavalry soon drove the outnumbered Federals over the ridgetops and down the other side to the safety of Fort Davidson. Wilson and his

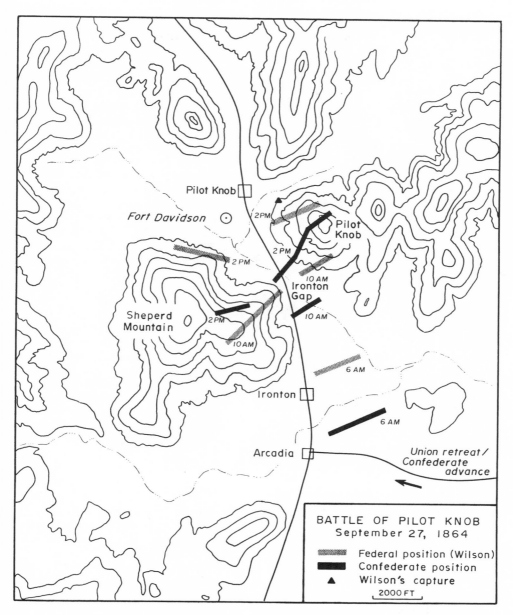

Troop positions during the Battle of Pilot Knob (author's collection).

cavalry were the last to retreat, coming in at noon. One side of Wilson's face and his jacket were still covered in dried blood from yesterday's fight. After listening to his report, Ewing ordered Wilson and his cavalry to establish a skirmish line along the northern flank of Pilot Mountain. Ewing then ordered the infantry that had come in earlier to deploy along the southern base of Shepherd Mountain. The men waited in their perilous positions, knowing they would

Captain Franz Dinger, 47th Missouri Infantry, as he appeared postwar (Iron County Historical Society).

the place of execution, and to that point the procession marched without music.

On the west side of the fort six posts had been set in the ground, each with a seat attached, and each tied with a strip of white cotton cloth, afterward used in bandaging the eyes of the prisoners. Fifty-four men were selected as the executioners, forty-four of them belonging to the 10th Kansas and ten to the 41st Missouri. Thirty-six of these composed the front firing party, eighteen being reserved in case they should not do the work effectually.

About three o'clock the prisoners arrived on the ground, and sat down, attached to the posts. They all appeared to be more or less affected, but, considering the circumstances, remained remarkably firm. Father Ward and Rev. Mr. McKim spoke to the men in their last moments, exhorting them to put their trust in God. The row of posts ranged north and south, and at the first on the north was Asa V. Ladd, on his left was [John] Nichols, next Harvey H. Blackburn, George [F.] Bunch, Charles W. Minniken and James W. Gates.[64]

be the first to face the full blow of the Rebel assault.[63]

Asa Ladd's Final Hour

At about two o'clock on Saturday afternoon, the six men were taken from the prison, placed in a covered wagon, and escorted to the place of execution by a detachment of the 10th Kansas, followed by a number of other soldiers, and by a few citizens. Fort No. 4, a short distance south of Lafayette Park, was selected as

Wilson's Capture

With the Federal forces confined to Fort Davidson, General Price ordered his artillery to the top of Shepherd Mountain, where they would have a sweeping view of the valley and the fort below. Four guns were pulled up the south side of the mountain, with a team of six mules and eight horses for each gun. They struggled for two hours pulling the guns up the boulder-strewn slopes and over rock ledges up to four feet in height.[65] Despite the commanding artillery position, General Price decided upon a full frontal assault on Fort Davidson following an artillery bombardment. A soldier in Price's army recalled that "we poor privates expected to see the enemy shelled out of that fort in double-quick time. It certainly could have been done in a few minutes; but instead of this, General Price and Fagan ordered a charge."[66]

Approximately 4,700 Confederate troops were deployed along the ridgelines of Shepherd and Pilot Mountains and in Ironton Gap. McCray's brigade, including the 15th Missouri Cavalry commanded by Colonel Timothy Reves, formed the extreme right of the Confederate line, just below the crest of Pilot Mountain. With the start of the artillery barrage at two o'clock in the afternoon, the Confederate line surged forward over the crests of Shepherd and Pilot Mountains. The advance was broken by the boulders, ravines, and fallen timber on the steep slopes. Major Wilson's skirmish line at the base of Pilot Mountain was made aware of the Confederate descent by Union shells passing over their heads and exploding high on the mountain.[67] They looked up to find McCray's brigade swarming down the hillside. Outnumbered ten to one, the Federals retreated slowly down the hillside. Captain Franz Dinger of the 47th Missouri Infantry wrote that Wilson ordered him to

go up higher on the hill about 300 yards from where I was and then ordered his [25] men still higher as skirmishers. He remained with me and my company.... We were attacked by the enemy on all sides and we took position in the hollow of the road leading to the pinnacle of the knob. We fired about 14 rounds but finding the return fire too strong for us, I ordered the men to fall back slowly to the foot of the hill and to keep firing as they did so. Maj. Wilson had 3 revolvers which he kept firing all the time at the advancing enemy.[68]

The Union line finally broke and scattered except for Major Wilson, Captain Dinger, and 15 men, who made a final stand behind an old steam mill at the foot of the mountain. Wilson, Dinger, and five men were "cut off at the mill and taken prisoners."[69]

Because of the irregular descent from Shepherd and Pilot Mountains, the Confederate brigades did not attack the fort in unison. This enabled the outnumbered Federal defenders to concentrate their fire on the nearest enemy. McCray's brigade was quickly pinned down in a dry stream bed on the open plain in front of the fort, where they remained for the rest of the fight. Parts of Clark's brigade and Cabell's brigade advanced through a "galling and destructive fire of artillery and musketry"[70] to advance within 20 yards of Fort Davidson's walls, only to be repulsed by the concentrated rifle fire of the Union soldiers on their knees behind the parapets. Other soldiers stood four to six deep and hurriedly reloaded the rifles for the men on the walls, thus maintaining a very rapid fire.[71] The Confederates could not withstand the deadly hail of bullets from the fort's walls, and finally turned and

Pilot Knob, viewed from the east wall of Fort Davidson. Confederate troops, including Colonel Reves and his men, descended this slope during the Battle of Pilot Knob (courtesy Dr. John L. Margreiter).

fled. Wilson and his men were being escorted to the rear of Price's army when

the repulsed and demoralized troops of Fagan's Division swept down the valley in a frantic stampede in which the guards over the prisoners joined, leaving Wilson and two enlisted men in this wild mob of Rebels. Major Wilson then turned back toward the fort with the two men, and was met by Lieutenant-Colonel John P. Bull, who had just ... left 42 [of his Arkansas regiment] dead or mortally wounded on the field. Though in full retreat with his men, Colonel Bull was composed enough to recognize a Federal major and two privates as a strange spectacle stemming their way in the contrary direction through the fleeing Rebel host, and at once took charge of them and turned them into the prison corral at Arcadia.[72]

The Death of Asa Ladd

Ladd and Blackburn sat with perfect calmness, with their eyes fixed on the ground, and did not speak. Nichols shed tears, which he wiped away with a red pocket handkerchief, and continued to weep until his eyes were bandaged. Nichols gave no sign of emotion at first, but sat with seeming indifference, scraping the ground with his heel. He asked one of the surgeons if there was any hope of a postponement, and being assured that there was none, he looked more serious, and frequently [expounded] "Lord, have mercy on my poor soul!" Again he said: "O, to think of the news that will go to father and mother!"

After the reading of the sentence by Col. Heinrichs, Minniken expressed a desire to say a few words. He said:

"Soldiers, and all of you who hear me,

View of Shepherd Mountain, looking southwest from Fort Davidson. The Confederate left struggled down this slope and charged unevenly across the open plain toward the fort (courtesy Dr. John L. Margreiter).

take warning from me. I have been a Confederate soldier four years, and have served my country faithfully. I am now to be shot for what other men have done, that I had no hand in, and know nothing about. I never was a guerrilla, and I am sorry to be shot for what I had nothing to do with, and what I am not guilty of. When I took a prisoner I always treated him kindly, and never harmed a man after he surrendered. I hope God will take me to his bosom when I am dead. O, Lord, be with me!"

While the sergeant was bandaging his eyes, Minnekin said "Sergeant, I don't blame you. I hope we will all meet in Heaven. Boys, when you kill me, kill me dead."

The eyes of all being bandaged, they bade each other farewell. "Good bye, George," said one; "Farewell Nichols," said another; "Good bye, Blackburn," uttered several, and two or three of them said, "Boys, farewell to you all, the Lord have mercy on our poor souls!"

The firing party was about ten paces

off. Some of the Kansas men appeared to be reluctant to fire upon the prisoners, but Captain Jones told them it was their duty; that they should have no hesitation, as these men had taken the life of many a Union man who was as innocent as themselves.

At the word, the thirty-six soldiers fired simultaneously, the discharge sounding like a single explosion. The aim of every man was true. One or two of the victims groaned, and Blackburn cried out: "Oh, kill me quick!" In five minutes they were all dead, their heads falling to one side, and their bodies swinging around to the sides of the posts, and being kept from falling by the pinions on their arms. Five of them were shot through the heart, and the sixth received three balls in his breast, dying almost instantly.

The execution was witnessed by several thousand spectators, most of them soldiers, and it was conducted in a manner highly creditable to those engaged in the performance of the disagreeable duty. The bodies were placed in plain painted coffins, and interred by Mr. Smithers.[73]

The Death of Major Wilson

Major Wilson, Captain Dinger, and the other Federal prisoners were confined to Arcadia Fort the night of September 27. The following day Dr. S. D. Carpenter, a Federal doctor from Pilot Knob, traveled to the prison camp and treated Major Wilson's head wound from two days before. The prisoners were marched to the rear of Price's army and followed Price through Richwood and St. Clair and on Sunday, October 2, "came to a place 10 miles west of Union, Mo."[74]

Captain Dinger recalled that "on the morning of October 3, we were called into line by a man who was called the Inspector General…. [He] rode up and down the line, asking where we were captured and our names."[75] Witnesses stated that each prisoner who gave his regiment as the 3rd Missouri State Militia Cavalry was ordered to step two paces to the front.[76] Major Wilson and five of his men — Corporal William W. Gourley and Privates William C. Grotts, William Scaggs, and John W. Shew (all members of Company I captured at Vandiver Farm), and Private John Holabaugh of Company K, captured with Wilson during the Battle of Pilot Knob — were the first to step forward. Other members of the 3rd MSM Cavalry further down the line, fearful that all 3rd MSM prisoners were going to be shot, gave different regiments. Privates Hiram Berry and Oscar O. Guilbert of Company I, by "hasty agreement between themselves, gave their regiment as the 17th Illinois Cavalry, and they were not asked to step forward. [Private] William Axford of Company H, was farther down the line among strangers, and when he noted that all members of his regiment were being stepped to the front, he spoke to the man next in line on his right, John Zoller of Company B, 14th Iowa Infantry, and said: 'They are going to shoot all the Third M.S.M. prisoners, what shall I do?' Zoller hastily replied: 'Give the same company and regiment that I do.'" Axford reported his regiment as the 14th Iowa and was passed by as the Inspector General moved down the line. A sixth unidentified soldier gave his command as the 3rd MSM, apparently thinking the first squad for parole was being selected, and unwittingly stepped forward to his doom.[77]

The men were ordered to the rear and the Inspector General told the officer of the guard to "put a double guard over that damned Major."[78] Another guard was posted on the road to watch for Colonel Reves's command, and when it came up to "hand these prisoners over to it."[79] Captain Dinger wrote that "I then went to Major Wilson who was just in the rear of me and he gave me his pocket-book, saying 'Capt., I have fallen into bad hands and I do not think I will see you again.' I then shook hands with him and went back to my place. Soon after I was paroled but Maj. Wilson and [his] men were taken away by a guard."[80] They were marched through an abandoned field, over a hill, and into the woods, and shortly afterwards some of the paroled prisoners heard a volley of musketry.

A Major for a Major

Federal authorities in St. Louis had yet to execute a Confederate major in retaliation for the death of Major Wilson. During the Battle of Mine Creek in Kansas on October 25, 1864, seven Confederate majors were captured, two of whom were field officers. The Confederate prisoners were marched over 100 miles to Warrensburg, Missouri, where they were loaded into stock cars and shipped to Gratiot Street Prison in St. Louis.[81] When it was decided that one of the two field majors would be executed, the prison guards drew straws[82] and on the morning of Tuesday, November 8, 1864, Major Enoch O. Wolf was summoned from the

Major Enoch O. Wolf, photographed postwar (*Confederate Veteran*).

prison where the Confederate officers were confined and taken to an anvil and a 12-pound ball and chain riveted to my ankle, and then my sentence read me as follows:

In retaliation for Major Wilson, Maj. Enoch O. Wolf, of Lieut. Col. B. Ford's battalion, Colonel T. R. Freeman's brigade, General Marmaduke's division, General Price's Army, shall be shot to death with musketry on Friday next [November 11th] between the hours of 9 and 11 o'clock.[83]

Major Wolf was confined to his cell under a strong guard. Later that day he wrote to General Rosecrans:

Now General, I have one favor to ask and it is with you to say whether it is fair or not. The favor is this: If this inhuman and unsoldier-like deed was committed will you please ask General Price to deliver the perpetrator of this crime, and if he turned Major Wilson over to this

Major General William Rosecrans (U.S. Army Military History Institute).

notorious bushwhacking Tim Reves to be executed, he certainly will make satisfaction by delivering up to the authorities the man who committed this inhuman crime.... I think these steps should be taken before you go further. I ask it as a soldier, as I asked it as a gentleman. I asked as an officer. I asked as a member of the Masonic fraternity. Excuse my bad writing.[84]

Major Wolf also wrote a letter to his wife Eviza and told her "that with the help of my Masonic friends she could raise our children all right." He had meetings and conversations with Reverend A. C. Osborn, a Baptist preacher, who baptized Wolf "in one of the large bathtubs in the bathroom at McDowell's College [Gratiot Street Prison]." Major Wolf asked Reverend Osborn to read his final letter to his wife to assure Federal authorities it was not of a contraband nature. "When he came to the part where I mentioned my Masonic friends he stopped reading and asked if I were a Mason. I made it plain to him that I was and he asked why I had not let it be known before. I told him I didn't know it would make any difference."[85] Osborn dropped the letter and rushed out of the prison to confer with other Masons in the city. On November 10, 1864, the day before Major Wolf's execution, President Lincoln received telegrams from James E. Yeatman, Able Barton, and P. L. Terry, all Masons from St. Louis, pleading clemency in the case of Major Wolf.[86] Later that day Lincoln sent the following telegram to Major General Rosecrans: "Suspend execution of Major Wolf until further order, & meanwhile, report to me on the case."[87]

The following day, November 11, Rosecrans wrote to Lincoln that

in compliance with your telegraphic orders of the 10th instant I transmit inclosed a printed statement of the case of Major Wolf, C. S. Army, and of the other rebels who were executed by my orders, for the purpose of teaching the enemy that if the laws of war and humanity are not sufficient to secure our prisoners from murder I will add to their force the motive of personal interest.... As to the policy of doing as I have done, I leave you to judge after reading the records of the case. All other motives having failed to secure my soldiers who have surrendered themselves prisoners of war from cold-blooded assassination or official murder by Price's command, I felt bound to appeal to the sense of personal security by declaring to these men that I should hold them individually responsible for the treatment of my troops while prisoners in their hands.[88]

After reading Rosecrans's reports, a telegram from President Lincoln dated November 19 informed Rosecrans that "I, without any particular knowledge of the facts, was induced by appeals for mercy, to order the suspension of his execution until further order ... this letter places the case again within your control, with the remark only that I wish you to do nothing merely for revenge, but that what you may do, shall be solely done with reference to the security of the future."[89]

A Letter of Condolence

Mrs. Amy Ladd:
    It becomes my painful duty to forward to you the last letter of your lamented husband, who was shot to

death on the 29th of October last at St. Louis, in retaliation for the murder of Maj. Wilson and six of his men by the Rebel Major Reves.

I attended your husband from the time he received his sentence to his death and am happy to say he bore his fate with Christian fortitude and resignation. At his request, I placed his testament, which he had carried with him all through the war, on his breast, in his coffin. God comfort you and his little children is the prayer of your apt servant.
Philip McKim
Chaplain[90]

Christmas Day, 1863

The killing of Major Wilson and his men by Colonel Timothy Reves has long been considered an act of barbarism, the climax to a long series of antagonistic encounters between Reves and Wilson's 3rd Missouri State Militia Cavalry. Their execution on the morning of October 3, 1864, has been assumed to be the retaliatory measure for the complete destruction of Doniphan, Reves's own home community, which was openly pro–Rebel and supportive of Reves and his men. "I must state for Colonel Reves," wrote General M. Jeff Thompson, that

> he was as good a man and soldier as any in the command, and his shooting of that party, was entirely justifiable, only it should have been done by such order and form that the retaliation would have been avoided. I solicited to have this party turned over to me that I might have them shot in due form, and Reves' men refrained from killing them for three days in hopes that I would get them but responsibilities of this kind

were not to our commander's liking, and they were turned over to Reves to guard, with a pretty full knowledge that they would be shot. I knew Reves' men, nearly every one of them, and the provocation was bitter, for I had seen the blackened ruins and lonely graves of Ripley County with my own eyes.[91]

It is likely, however, that the fate of Major Wilson and his men, after falling into Timothy Reves's hands, was shaped on Christmas Day, 1863. Three days earlier, on the 22nd of December, Reves's command captured an entire company of the 3rd MSM Cavalry at Centerville, in nearby Reynolds County. "Company C is captured, excepting a few men," wrote Colonel R. G. Woodson, then commander of the 3rd Subdistrict at Pilot Knob.

> They were surprised, building stables. No fight, a few scattering shots, and a few wounded; none killed…. I find the catastrophe … much aggravated, if not occasioned, by carelessness…. The facts that the enemy's means of information are so much superior to ours, that he avoided roads for a long distance below, thus escaping detection by a patrol party there to ascertain the state of affairs and report, and that making a large circuit he came in from the west across the hills, and not by any road, with his advance dressed in Federal uniforms, may afford some excuse.[92]

After capturing Company C, Reves's command immediately moved out to the south, setting up camp on Forche Creek, near Pulliam Spring, south of Doniphan near the Arkansas line. Major Wilson, with instructions to "follow him to hell,"[93] left Pilot Knob with 200 men about ten o'clock in the morning on December 23 and headed south. On December 25, Christmas Day, they "passed through Doniphan, taking a southwesterly direction toward the Arkansas line. Eight miles from Doniphan, I captured two pickets; two miles farther I captured one other post, and still 2 miles farther on came upon a rolling picket or patrol, and run them off the road, capturing 1 and compelling him to lead us to the camp of Reves."[94]

On Christmas Day Reves's men were preparing a holiday celebration. "Four or five preachers were in attendance and a Christmas preaching was carried on for the cavalrymen, their families, and most of the people living in the neighborhood. A Christmas meal was prepared by the Regimental messes."[95] Local residents serving in other Confederate units were also attending. "Old man Reves ... preached to them [captured] Yankees a whole afternoon," wrote a local resident. "He sure could get excited about preaching."[96]

According to Wilson's report, after arriving at the camp, he divided [his] men into two columns, and

> charged upon them with my whole force. The enemy fired, turned, and threw down their arms and fled, with the exception of 30 or 35, and they were riddled with bullets or pierced through with the saber almost instantly. The enemy lost in killed about 30; mortally wounded, 3; slightly 2; total killed and wounded, 35. Prisoners captured, 112; horses, besides those of Company C, 75; also all their arms, ammunition, and camp equipage.... There was no loss on our side in killed or wounded.[97]

Confederate accounts indicate arms were stacked and the group was prepar-

ing to eat their meal when the Federals attacked from all sides. In addition to the Confederate casualties, over 60 civilians, many of them women and children, were killed or wounded during the attack.[98, 99] Two of the women killed were Sarah Ponder, wife of Abner J. Ponder, and Emaline Ponder, wife of Daniel MacKenzie Crockett Ponder, two soldiers in Reves's command. A. J. Ponder's five-year-old daughter, Louisa, was also shot to death.[100] According to members of Doniphan's Confederate Veterans Camp, the Union soldiers ate the Christmas meal and then moved out with the prisoners and all the horses, leaving the wounded behind. "The ranks of the regiment were swelled by recruits anxious to avenge the deaths of their kin or friends, a number sufficient to overcome the loss from killed or captured."[101]

Major Wilson's Christmas Day attack was successful in wrecking Colonel Reves's command, but the killing of the civilians enraged Ripley County. It is not known if Wilson was aware of their presence when he deployed his troops in the heavy brush around the camp. The troops charged with guns firing and killed Confederates and family members alike as they mingled before their Christmas meal. Wilson's official report of the incident does not mention civilian casualties, which must be construed as an attempt to keep the fact from the official record.[102]

Ripley County, already ravaged by three years of guerrilla warfare and bushwhacking, became more protective of Reves, replenishing his command and increasing resistance to Federal authority in the area. This may have compelled Wilson to have his troops burn

Daniel MacKenzie Crockett Ponder (courtesy Jerry Ponder).

and his men marched with the Confederate column, strongly guarded by the 15th Missouri Cavalry. Colonel T. J. Oliphant remembered that

a body of men, who had charge of them, with Col. Reves at the head, turned from the main road.... The march of the prisoners was exceeding quiet and slow. They passed suddenly into the bed of a creek and on to the other side.... While thus stopped, Col. Reves addressed Maj. Wilson and told him that he had been ordered by Gen. Price to take them out and shoot them, when Maj. Wilson, looking straight into the eye of Col. Reves, said "You do not mean to say that you are going to shoot us without a trial?" To which Col. Reves replied, "You have been tried, and such are my orders," and ordered "forward." Passing on a short distance ... a halt was ordered and the prisoners placed close to the bottom of [a] swag, and the men detailed to shoot stationed above them, with a strong guard on the other side. When they were placed in position to be shot, [a sixteen year old] boy began to cry and take on at a terrible rate, saying "I have a widowed mother in Arkansas, and she is a good southern woman, and these men forced me to go with them!" My sympathy was so aroused that I rode around to where the colonel was sitting on his horse, and said "Colonel, it looks hard to shoot that boy." To which he replied, "Yes; but he is in bad company, and such are my orders." ...Before the order to fire was given, Maj. Wilson and the men were asked "if they had anything to say" and

Doniphan in September of 1864. The civilian deaths during the Christmas Day attack, combined with the wanton destruction of Doniphan, made the hatred for Major Wilson and the 3rd MSM complete. When he and his men were separated from the other prisoners on October 3 to be turned over to Reves, his fate must have become clear to him. He said farewell to Captain Dinger, saying that he had "fallen into bad hands" and would not see him again. Wilson none but the boy said anything, and he nothing more than I have stated. Maj. Wilson took his hat off and laid it on the ground in front of him, and he and the five others stood facing the detail, apparently without a tremor, but the boy continued his cry. When the fire was ordered, Maj. Wilson was shot dead with many bullets. All were shot to the ground except the boy, who stood untouched, and a peremptory order was given to shoot again, when he fell dead. The men were stripped of their clothing, such as could be used as trophies, and especially Maj. Wilson, and they were left where they fell.[103]

Wilson's death may have avenged the hardships inflicted on Ripley County by the 3rd Missouri State Militia Cavalry, but after Price's raid the Federal authorities were more determined than ever to hunt down Colonel Reves and the 15th Missouri Cavalry for the murder of seven prisoners of war.

Abner J. Ponder (courtesy Jerry Ponder).

Price's Retreat

General Price's attack on Fort Davidson failed. The Confederate descent from Shepherd and Pilot Mountains was broken and irregular, and the troops did not charge in unison across the open plain in front of the fort. With the exception of General Cabell's hard-fighting brigade of Arkansas cavalry, the attackers gave up early and saved themselves from the concentrated rifle fire, many of them taking shelter in a dry creek bed. Cabell's men advanced bravely to the fort's walls, but were finally driven back by hand grenades

Site of the Christmas Day fight on Forche Creek, 1863. It was here that Major Wilson's men attacked Colonel Reves's camp, killing a number of women and children (courtesy Jerry Ponder).

hurled into the Rebel mass, which blew men above the parapet walls. Following Cabell's final retreat, Price's army withdrew towards Ironton for the night.[104]

General Price was incensed by the day's action—his forces had not taken the fort, and over 500 of the 4,700 participants lay dead or wounded on the field, many of them Cabell's men. Federal losses during the fight were 77 killed or wounded and 129 missing (most of them skirmishers cut off during the initial advance, including Major Wilson) out of a fighting force of 1,500 men.[105]

Fearing the attack would be renewed in the morning with a heavy artillery bombardment, General Ewing decided to evacuate Fort Davidson that night. The Federal troops moved out at one o'clock in the morning. Commands were whispered from man to man. Horses were walked across the drawbridge, which was covered by straw and blankets to deaden the sound of their passage. Remarkably, they passed near Rebel campfires and pickets without challenge, being mistaken for Confederates changing position. A squad of men remained behind and ignited the ammunition magazine at 3:30 in the morning. The huge explosion, which threw timbers, guns, and debris hundreds of feet into the air, was assumed by Confederate commanders to be a catastrophic accident within the fort's walls.[106, 107, 108]

The next morning, September 28,

Price was enraged to discover the Federals had escaped, and sent Generals Marmaduke and Shelby in pursuit. Despite some rear-guard actions, Ewing reached Leasburg on September 29 after marching 66 miles in 39 hours. He hurriedly erected fortifications. The pursuing Confederates withdrew and rejoined Price's army.

The fight at Pilot Knob was a costly defeat. Price lost over 500 of his veteran cavalry, and the ill-conceived battle plan ruined the army's confidence in their commanders. Ewing delayed Price's advance on St. Louis long enough to enable the reinforcement of that city by Federal troops under General A. J. Smith. "After caring for our wounded and burying our dead," wrote one of Price's men, "we resumed our march, following the Missouri River. Constantly for twenty days succeeding some part of our command was engaged with the enemy."[109] The army moved west along the southern bank of the Missouri River, tearing up railroad and burning bridges. The march was also marked by the indiscriminate killing of Federal prisoners and widespread looting and pillaging.

General Price arrived in Boonville on October 10, 1864. He wrote that "old and young, men, women, and children, vied in their salutation and in ministering to the wants and comforts of my wearied and war-torn soldiers."[110] An officer recalled "the entire army was camped in and around the town.... The bushwhackers began to pour in. Anderson ["Bloody Bill"] ... brought probably three hundred men. Quantrell came over to compare notes, and the hitherto quiet town of Boonville put on its holiday attire."[111] Price's recognition of Quantrell

and Anderson (he awarded Anderson a captaincy and attached him to his command), two ruthless killers who murdered and mutilated soldiers and citizens alike, shocked Missouri Unionists. Price tarried at Boonville for three days "for no other reason than to let his soldiers have a good time with the home folks."[112]

Federal elements began to unite into a more cohesive force, and resistance to Price's march began to stiffen. Price was caught in a costly rear-guard action at The Battle of Mine Creek on October 25, 1864. Spirited cavalry charges (including Lt. Col. Frederick Benteen's 10th Missouri Cavalry) routed Marmaduke's forces and captured a number of prisoners, including Generals Marmaduke and Cabell and Major Enoch O. Wolf.[113] The defeat ruined what little morale the army had left, and many soldiers deserted to return home. Burning wagons and other abandoned property were left behind to facilitate the march.[114] Federal reports indicated that

> Price is now entering a mountainous country very destitute of supplies, and his men are actually falling dead of starvation in his rear.... He has destroyed most of his train and is very destitute, but all of his men being mounted he continues to make rapid progress.... His troops are so destitute of provisions ... the elm trees for miles had been stripped to furnish food for the starving multitude.[115]

Federal pursuit lessened following the Battle of Mine Creek. Price began to disassemble his army on November 2, ordering units into northern Arkansas.[116] Colonel McCray and his

Configuration of the south-central United States during the Civil War (author's collection).

men (including Timothy Reves) left on November 3 for Jacksonport, Arkansas. Price and his remaining army, in a torturous detour around the Federal stronghold at Fort Smith, Arkansas, entered Indian Territory on November 5. A few days later Cabell's Brigade was ordered to Spring Hill, Arkansas. Price's men "endured the severest privations and sufferings" during the march. An officer reported that "for twenty five days our animals were without salt, frequently issued in insufficient quantities, and for three days were without food at all. The loss in animals was very heavy."[117]

The army reached Clarksville, Texas, on November 28, and arrived at Laynesport, Arkansas, on December 2, 1864. Price's raid was over.

McCray's Brigade arrived in Jacksonport, Arkansas, on November 10, 1864. Reves and his men returned to their activities along the Missouri/Arkansas border. An attack by a Federal patrol on January 10, 1865, "came near to capturing Reves ... one captain that was with him [was] killed; captured his quartermaster. Reves escaped, half dressed, by getting into the swamp and swimming Black River."[118] The streams were high and overflowing, and a Federal officer noted "the whole face of the country for eight miles ... [was covered] with water from two to three feet deep, through which the command had to march and break their way through ice from one and a half to two inches thick."[119] A week later Reves was attacked again on Cherokee Bay and driven into the swamps.[120] Reves found it impossible to keep enough men together to maintain an effective fighting force—they were demoralized, their families impoverished,

and the countryside devastated. Reves spent the remaining months of the war on the run from Federal patrols anxious to avenge the death of Major Wilson.

Colonel Reves's command was with Brigadier General M. Jeff Thompson when he and over 7,000 men surrendered to Union forces in northern Arkansas in May 1865. "The only person that presented himself that we declined to parole was Col. Tim. Reves, Fifteenth Missouri Cavalry," wrote Lieutenant-Colonel C. W. Davis. "He is the officer that ordered the shooting of Major Wilson and six of his men in the fall of 1864, after they had surrendered."[121]

Epilogue

Reves lived an apparently quiet life as a Baptist minister in Ripley County following the war. As an elder with the Cane Creek Association of United Missionary Baptists,[122] he baptized over 80 persons and organized five new churches in northeastern Arkansas and Butler, Carter, and Ripley Counties, Missouri. In October of 1867 he married a widow from Carter County. Timothy Reves died at the age of 63 on March 13, 1885, and was buried on his farm a few miles north of Doniphan. His grave is near the junction of Missouri Highway 21 and Ripley County Highway K, and is marked by a headstone that reads:

> Separation is our lot
> Meeting is our gain...

Sometime after the war he may have changed the spelling of his name to Reeves, as it appears on his headstone.

Amy Ladd did not receive Asa's

Gravesite of Colonel Timothy Reves (courtesy Jerry Ponder).

letter until after the war. Having apparently heard of her husband's fate, Amy had decided to leave the farm. The family's possessions were loaded into two wagons, and a man was hired to drive the other wagon. As Asa had feared, the rainy season had begun, and the St. Francis River was high. As they attempted the perilous crossing one of the wagons was swept away, the team of oxen drowned, and the possessions lost. The Ladd family continued south in the single wagon and settled in Fulton County, Arkansas, near Amy's twin sister, Namy. There she raised her seven children and never remarried. Ransom Ladd, Asa's father, traveled to Gratiot Street Prison after the war to retrieve his son's belongings, where he discovered Asa's farewell letters. Mr. Ladd kept the letters in the family bible until Amy could be located. Amy Ladd lived with her children until she died around the year 1900.[123]

Following his pardon by President Lincoln, Major Enoch O. Wolf remained at Gratiot Street Prison for two months before being transferred to the prison on Johnson's Island in Lake Erie. Wolf was released in the spring of 1865 and returned to his farm near Franklin, Arkansas. He served in the state legislature and was a sheriff in Fulton County, Arkansas. Major Wolf died on October 20, 1910, at the age of 83, survived by his wife and seven children. [124, 125]

Private John A. Ferguson, who was spared execution by the late substitution of George F. Bunch, died of "phthisis pulmo" on April 5, 1865, at the U.S. General Prison Hospital in St. Louis. The war ended four days later.[126]

Reverend Phillip McKim, an Irishman who had journeyed to New York City at the age of 17 was assistant minister to the Grace Episcopal Church in St. Louis during the war, and served as chaplain for the U.S. Army. Reverend McKim married Jennie Langdon in Hannibal, Missouri, on April 26, 1866. He was one of the few clergymen who remained in St. Louis during the summer of 1866 to minister the sick during a deadly cholera outbreak. His health failing, he left Grace Church in St. Louis in 1868 for the "country," founding churches in Illinois, Ohio, Wisconsin, Minnesota, Iowa, and Nebraska from 1868 to 1891. Reverend McKim died on July 17, 1897, while a Missionary at Trinity Church in Norfolk, Nebraska. He was survived by his wife Jennie and four children. [127, 128, 129]

Captain Franz Dinger resided in Ironton, Missouri, when he joined the Federal service. His wife Amelia listened to the frightening sounds of the Battle of Pilot Knob from the cellar of their home. When she emerged after the battle, she fainted at the sight of the Confederate casualties strewn before her (the house was later used as a temporary field hospital). Captain Dinger received his license to practice law in 1866, and served as mayor, justice of the peace, and county judge. He and his wife raised ten children. Captain Dinger died in 1893 at the age of 61.

William Leeper served with the 3rd Missouri State Militia cavalry until the end of the war. Accused of wanton killing and looting, he was hated by the largely pro–Confederate southern

The final resting place of Private Asa V. Ladd, Jefferson Barracks Cemetery, St. Louis, Missouri (courtesy Charles Staats II).

The Confederate section in the Jefferson Barracks Cemetery, St. Louis, Missouri (courtesy Charles Staats II).

counties. He resided in Wayne County after the war and was successful as a surveyor, lawyer, state representative, prosecuting attorney, and banker. He and his wife raised 14 children. The community of Leeper, Missouri, was named in his honor.

Refusing to surrender at the end of the war, generals Price and Shelby, with a band of loyal soldiers, rode southward into Mexico to support Emperor Maximilian. When that government collapsed, Price returned to St. Louis in 1866 and died there the following year, disillusioned and impoverished. Shelby also returned to Missouri, and was appointed a U.S. Marshal by President Cleveland in 1893.[130, 131]

Major James Wilson is buried in Troy, Missouri. A monument was erected over his grave in 1870 by friends and fellow officers. The marker reads "Preserve What He Gave His Life to Defend: Our Nationality." His younger brother John served as the Lincoln County assessor until his premature death in 1877 at the age of 38, leaving behind an "aged mother, whose support and comfort he was."[132]

Privates Asa V. Ladd, James W. Gates, George F. Bunch, Harvey H. Blackburn, John Nichols, and Charles W. Minnekin now rest in graves 4605–4610 in Section 21, Jefferson Barracks National Cemetery, St. Louis, Missouri.

Postscript

Despite exhaustive efforts to locate primary, first-person source material documenting the casualties during the Christmas Day fight between Reves and Wilson, only three "secondary" sources could be found. The first is the Ponder family history, which indicates three female members in that family died on Christmas Day, 1863. The second is a story about the battle by Dr. John Hume, a well-respected local historian who cited interviews with surviving Confederate veterans who participated in the engagement. The description of the fight in this story was taken largely from Dr. Hume's account. The third is an 1889 interview with Mrs. Washington Harris, who indicated 62 women and children were killed. She attended the "burying" in Doniphan.

I continue to seek any information that would further document the tragedies of that Christmas Day in 1863.

More from Missouri: Brother Against Brother

When the war broke out the loyalties of the Wilson family were divided. They had moved west from Maryland in 1852 and settled in Lincoln County, Missouri, near Millwood. Mr. James Wilson was a short, fierce man and an ardent secessionist. According to local history, Mr. Wilson was the only Southern sympathizer in the area who was permitted by the militia to keep his rifle.[133] His eldest son and namesake, James, did not share his family's Rebel convictions and enlisted in the Union Army as a private in 1861, severing "al-

most all ties that bound him to family and home."[134] His next son, John, joined the Confederate Army as a member of the 2nd Missouri infantry. John lost his left arm at the Battle of Corinth, Mississippi, and was captured and paroled during the fall of Vicksburg in 1863. James was promoted to major of the 3rd Missouri State Militia cavalry in 1863 and commanded the military subdistrict at Pilot Knob. The father of two young sons, he was divorced from his wife Margaret in September of 1864. A few days later Major Wilson was captured by the enemy after fighting bravely during the Battle of Pilot Knob, only to be executed by Timothy Reves's men on October 3, 1864.[135]

The Swamp

Cherokee Bay was an extensive, swampy lowland between the Black and Current Rivers along the Missouri/ Arkansas border. It was a hideout for Timothy Reves and his 15th Missouri cavalry, which often eluded Union forces by disappearing into the swamps. Confederate camps were located on patches of high ground deep in the "Bay," surrounded for miles by dense swamp and standing water. Regarded as miserable, snake-infested territory, logging and agriculture drained and cleared the area in the post–Civil War years.

Revenge for Doniphan

Shortly before sunrise on September 20, 1864, Sergeant Simon U. Branstetter and the rest of Lieutenant Eric

Facing south toward the Black River, in the southwestern corner of Butler County. The site was once the center of Cherokee Bay (photographs by the author).

Pape's 86 men were preparing to ride to the Federal outpost at Patterson, Missouri. The day before, Pape's command from the 3rd Missouri State Militia cavalry had routed a Confederate patrol from Doniphan, and then proceeded to burn the community to the ground. Doniphan was openly pro–Rebel and harbored the Confederate "guerrilla" Tim Reves and his 15th Missouri cavalry. As the Federal soldiers rode northward from Doniphan they burned more homes along the route. At sunset they camped at Vandiver's Farm near Ponder's Mill on the Black River, about 20 miles north of Doniphan. Pape put out only a camp guard that night, despite Branstetter's appeal to throw out pickets "some distance from our camp, for I was sure that we were right in the face of Price's army."

As the woods grew light and the Federals were saddling their horses, they were attacked on all sides by 150 Confederates under the command of Lieutenant Colonel Rector Johnson, who had been ordered by General J. O. Shelby to overtake the Union raiders. Pape's command charged through the cross fire with a heavy loss. Sergeant Branstetter's horse was shot down from under him, and he found himself surrounded by Confederates. Upon surrendering his pistol, one of the Confederate soldiers shot him from point blank range, the ball tearing through his right breast and exiting just below the shoulder blade, knocking him senseless to the ground. When Branstetter regained consciousness he found "a large stream of blood squirting from my mouth with every breath and a circle of rebels around me." They stripped him

naked of all his clothing except his shirt, which was too blood-soaked for anyone to wear.

They left Branstetter to feed their horses and have some breakfast. After they were finished, Branstetter heard a command to turn out a grave-digging squad for the "one dead Fed." After digging a shallow grave, they came to pick up Branstetter when one remarked "Why, that damned Fed ain't dead enough yet to bury!" The Confederates then argued about killing him with one more shot, but they were prevented by the "oldest man of the party, who was dressed in a brown suit of clothes, broad brimmed slouched hat and had long whiskers flowing over his breast." The Rebels built a crude lean-to of fence rails over him so he could be somewhat protected in his last few minutes or hours. Fearing they would shoot him if he seemed more alive than dead, Branstetter feigned unconsciousness. Being naked and having lost much blood, it took his greatest effort to keep from shivering in the cold morning air. The Confederate band finally rode off, the "hoof beats of their horses and the jangling of their sabers dying down in the distance, and all was still ... except the rustling of the breeze and the singing of the birds above in the branches."

After an hour of lying motionless under the rails, Branstetter got up and staggered away into the woods. He walked nearly ten hours across the rocky ground, bathing his wound and his torn and bleeding feet in the streams that he crossed. Near sunset he followed a cow path down to the valley farms below, where he approached the nearest residence. The owner, a Butler County judge named Scott, "at once took me into the house and made a pallet by the fire." Judge Scott sent his son to summon the local doctor, who, being a strong Rebel sympathizer, refused to treat the Yankee soldier. The Scott family stayed up with Branstetter that night until nearly four o'clock in the morning, tending his wound.

The following day General Fagan's division of Price's army marched by Judge Scott's house early in the morning, and the Rebels soon discovered Branstetter, "dismounting and running into the house to see me. Judge Scott ... instructed me to appear just as nearly dead as I could in order that some sympathy might be excited in the minds or hearts of Rebels who would necessarily view me during the day.... Many of them cursed me and abused me vilely, and some of them suggested to Judge Scott that he carry me outside and let them shoot me and finish the job, but he declined to do this, saying that I might lie in his house and die where I was." Branstetter appealed to Judge Scott to inquire about a parole from General Price, which was granted and delivered through his chief of staff. The rear of Price's army camped near Judge Scott's house that night and fed his entire corn crop to their horses.

Sergeant Branstetter began his journey home on September 30, only ten days after receiving his wound, with a supply of fresh corn bread baked by Mrs. Scott. Dressed in old clothes from the Scotts and a tattered coat from an Irish family with whom he spent his first night, Branstetter traveled cross-country towards Patterson, "playing the part of a Rebel soldier who had been sick and left behind." After learning Pilot Knob had been captured by Price, he turned east towards Cape Girardeau, passing through Hog Eye and Dallas. He arrived in Jackson on October 3 and was relieved to find it under Union control. Equipped with a civilian guide and a Federal mule, Sergeant Branstetter arrived at the Federal hospital in Cape Girardeau shortly thereafter.[136]

Branstetter was later transferred to a hospital in St. Louis, where he remained for a month. Afterwards he returned home on leave of absence until December 18, 1864, when he rejoined his regiment. During this time he married Nancy Jane Chamberlain on November 27. After the war he returned to his home near Vandalia, Missouri, where he farmed, raised livestock, and owned a general store. He and his wife Nancy raised eight children. Simon Branstetter died at the age of 91 on December 15, 1932.[137]

Scenes from Gratiot Street Prison

Originally a medical college built by Dr. Joseph Nash McDowell in the 1850s, Gratiot Street Prison in St. Louis held Confederate prisoners, Union army deserters, and citizens considered disloyal, including women and children. Built with massive stone walls and large windows that provided light and air, the building could hold 500 safely but frequently held over twice that number. Many escape attempts occurred, and twice the prisoners set the prison on fire.

Captain Griffin Frost was captured by Federal forces on November 8, 1862, in Carroll County, Arkansas. After being briefly held in Springfield, Missouri, Captain Frost was transferred to Gratiot Street Prison in January 1863. After the war he returned home to Quincy, Illinois, where he published an account of his imprisonment for his friends. The following excerpts from his journal describe life in Gratiot Street Prison.

> January 5. There are now about eight hundred prisoners in Gratiot and more coming in every day from all parts of the country. We are allowed only two meals a day, and it keeps the cooks busy to get through with them by dark. Some two or three hundred eat at a time, and the tin plates and cups are never washed from the first to last table. For breakfast we have one-fifth of a loaf of baker's bread, a small portion of bacon, and a tin cup of stuff they call coffee. For dinner the same amount of bread, a hunk of beef, and a pint of water the beef was boiled in, which is called soup, and sometimes a couple of boiled potatos all dished up and portioned out with the hands, knives, forks, and spoons not being allowed....
>
> January 7. Received orders to-day to move ourselves and baggage to the officer's quarters. Find it a great improvement on the old position—much cleaner and not so crowded. There are eight of us in a room sixteen feet square.... We have the privilege of using knives, forks, and spoons, which we prefer to the finger plan in vogue below....
>
> January 8. We have a good view from the windows, where we stand and watch for the Southern ladies to pass. God bless them! They always give us a pleasant smile; it is like a glimpse of

> heaven to look in their dear, sympathizing faces.
>
> January 14. To-day we are cooped up in our den, not allowed even to put our heads out of the windows—if we do the guard are ordered to shoot us. One of their own men was put in here for some offence, probably without knowing of the order, looked out of the window, when the guard fired and the poor wretch fell dead. Our consolation was, that it was not one of us, but it looked hard to see even an enemy killed in that way.
>
> March 13, 1863. Five Confederate officers made their escape this morning, and because [we] could not tell how it occurred we were thrown into the strong room and locked up....
>
> March 18. Several citizens were brought in while I was in lock-up. One of them—Dr. Merwin, received the gratifying intelligence that his property had been confiscated, and would be used for the benefit of the United States government. I thought he would go crazy when he heard it, he was so filled with rage and indignation. They won't allow his wife to come near the prison. I feel sorry for him; his offence is corresponding with his friends in Dixie.[138]

Retaliation in Palmyra

Another act of Federal retaliation that enraged the pro–Confederate populace occurred in Palmyra, Missouri, on October 18, 1862.

As were many towns in Missouri, Palmyra was bitterly divided between Unionists and Confederate sympathizers. One of the foremost Unionists in the community was a man named Andrew Allsman, a former member of the 3rd Missouri cavalry who had retired from active duty at the age of 60.

Allsman continued to serve the Federal government in a variety of ways, including informing on "disloyal" citizens and guiding Federal patrols. Allsman thus "won the bitter hatred of all the rebels in this city and vicinity."

When Confederate General Joseph C. Porter and his men occupied Palmyra briefly in the fall of 1862, Allsman quickly disappeared and was not heard from again. "Whether he was stabbed at midnight by the dagger of the assassin, or shot at midday by the rifle of the guerrilla; whether he was hung ... or left as food for hogs to fatten upon ... we know not."

Upon learning of the abduction of Allsman, Federal General John McNeil informed Porter on October 8, 1862, that "unless said Andrew Allsman is returned, unharmed, to his family within ten days from [this] date, ten men, who have belonged to your band ... and who are now in custody ... will be shot as a meet reward for their crimes."

The ten days elapsed with no word from Porter of Allsman, and on October 18th "a little after 11 a.m. ... three Government wagons drove to the jail; one contained four and each of the others three rough board coffins." The condemned Rebel prisoners rode on the coffins in the wagons to the fair grounds; half a mile east of Palmyra. The coffins were removed from the wagons and placed in a row on the ground. A firing squad consisting of 30 soldiers from the 2nd Missouri State Militia was drawn up in a single line facing the coffins.

The doomed men were Captain Thomas A. Snider and privates Willis Baker, Thomas Humston, Lewis Wade, Morgan Bixler, Herbert Hudson, John

M. Wade, Marion Lair, Eleazer Lake, and Kiram Smith. "The men knealt upon the grass between their coffins and the soldiers, while the Rev. R. M. Rhodes offered up a prayer. At the conclusion of this, each prisoner took his seat upon the foot of his coffin."

Captain Snider was "elegantly attired in a suit of black broadcloth with a white vest ... and beautiful hair rolled down upon his shoulders." Two of the other Rebels accepted blindfolds. At the command to fire, the rifles discharged unevenly, only killing three of the men instantly. Captain Snider sprang forward from his coffin, shot through the heart. The wounded were then dispatched by soldiers who moved in with revolvers.[139]

The Arrival of "Mrs. Wolf"

The morning of Major Wolf's execution dawned with no word yet received from President Lincoln on his behalf. The commander of the prison informed him that his wife had arrived and wished to see him. Major Wolf was pleased with the news, as he was "anxiously awaiting the time when I would see my sweet wife for the last time in this world." When the cell door was opened, Wolf was surprised to not see his wife but a young woman "dressed like a butterfly" who rushed to him exclaiming "My dear husband! My dear husband!" She threw her arms around his neck and whispered that he should claim her as his wife. "My nerve through life will compare with any man's," wrote Major Wolf, "but this knocked all the nerve out of me, but I could not tell a lie just before I died."[140] The woman was taken away in handcuffs and imprisoned as a spy. Shortly afterwards a telegram from President Lincoln was announced, staying the execution of Major Wolf.

The beautiful young lady, 18 to 20 years of age, was identified as Kate Batie, the wife of a Missouri guerrilla named Tuck Batie. She had arrived in St. Louis the previous day to claim Wolf as her husband, a ploy intended to spare his life. Major Wolf was called to testify during her trial. The prosecutors, using statements made by Wolf regarding his wife and five children upon his capture, told her "she looked young to be the mother of five children and she told them three were children of a former wife. But I had told them that I had never been married before, and they had her completely trapped."[141]

After her trial President Lincoln telegraphed General Grenville M. Dodge in St. Louis that "if Mrs. Beattie, *alias* Mrs. Wolf, shall be sentenced to death, notify me, and postpone execution till further order." General Dodge responded that she had already been sent to "her friends in the Rebel lines."[142] Major Wolf recalled that he saw her several years after the war and "she still bore on her wrists scars caused by the sores made by the handcuffs around her wrists."[143]

Confederates in Blue

Accounts of Price's raid through Missouri contain numerous references to Confederate soldiers wearing Federal uniforms. This was particularly effective in the hit-and-run tactics of smaller Confederate forces such as Colonel

Reves's 15th Missouri cavalry, who often dressed his advance in blue. The roads of southeastern Missouri were traveled by bushwhackers, guerrillas, and ruffians wearing Federal cavalry coats. It was also a tactic commonly used by the murderous guerrilla bands of Anderson, Quantrill, Thrailkill, and Todd. Thus Union troops were partial toward immediately executing any of the enemy captured in blue uniforms.

In a letter carried to Federal authorities by Major Enoch O. Wolf during a prisoner exchange in 1864, Confederate Colonel T. R. Freeman wrote:[144]

> You informed me in your last communication that you were ordered to put to death all Confederate soldiers wearing the uniform of the U.S. Army. This cannot be a general order, or it is not always executed, for there are hundreds of our Confederate prisoners who have been taken in that uniform and afterward exchanged. Besides, the laws of war have always allowed one army to deceive another either by wearing the enemy's uniform or hoisting its flag. Furthermore, your own soldiers, when on the march through the country, frequently send their advance dressed in citizen's clothing for the purpose of deceiving us or the citizens, and if you should put to death all Confederate soldiers dressed in Federal uniform you could not blame me for putting to death all Federal soldiers taken without their entire uniform.

Colonel R. R. Livingston, commander of the District of Northeastern Arkansas at Batesville, returned the following reply with Major Wolf:[145]

> I have no alternative in regard to the wearing of Federal uniforms by the enemies of the United States. When our men are caught wearing your uniforms

they must stand the consequences, but where they are in their own regular uniform ... I expect you will treat them kindly ... as your own men are treated by us ... I do not object to your killing my men if you catch them in Confederate uniform, and will carry out my orders with regard to all confederates wearing the uniform of the United States.

When General Price invaded Missouri his men were poorly clothed and equipped. As in the case of Sergeant Simon Branstetter, they frequently stripped the dead and wounded for better clothing and boots. As the campaign wore on into October and November the troops faced colder weather. When Price occupied Glasgow, Missouri, on October 15, he seized 1,000 new suits of Federal cavalry clothing, which were distributed among his men. Ten days later, during the Battle of Little Osage Creek, Price's forces were routed and over 1,000 prisoners captured. "A number of prisoners taken in this fight were dressed in our uniform," wrote a Federal officer, "and in obedience to existing orders from department headquarters, and the usages of war, they were executed instanter, while those taken in Confederate uniform were recognized and treated as prisoners of war."[146]

Thus new coats of Federal blue, which helped protect Confederate soldiers from rain and snow on the march, led to their deaths after being captured during the last major engagement of Price's campaign.

IV

Rebel Resort of the Dead: The History of General Hospital Number One, Kittrell's Springs, North Carolina

William B. Kennedy left his home in Hallsville at age 24 and enlisted in the Confederate Army in June 1861 "for the War."[1] On October 27, 1864, Private Kennedy and the 1st North Carolina Cavalry (9th Regiment of North Carolina State Troops) were engaged in the battle of Boydton Plank Road, Virginia, one of the many actions of General U. S. Grant's Petersburg campaign. Grant ordered the advance of an estimated 43,000 Federal troops across Hatcher's Run in an attempt to cut the Boydton Plank Road and the Southside Railroad, two open lines to the entrenched Confederate center. The movement began in the gloom of the dark and rainy morning of October 27. By noon, General Winfield S. Hancock with two divisions of troops and Major General David Gregg's division of cavalry had reached the Boydton Plank Road. As Gregg began his advance along the Plank Road, he was met by the 1st and 5th Regiments of North Carolina Cavalry (elements of Major General Fitzhugh Lee's cavalry division) and, according to one member of the 1st North Carolina, "quickly then the battle was on in all its fury ... all along the line everywhere the fighting was terrific and furious."[2] Major General Wade Hampton, who commanded the Confederate cavalry during the battle, reported "Lee attacked with great spirit, driving the enemy rapidly and handsomely."[3]

The Confederate cemetery at Kittrell, North Carolina (photograph by the author).

The battle continued until nightfall, steady musket fire flashing across the darkening countryside. Stopped by a hard-fighting force of Confederates estimated at 20,000 in number, Hancock's troops retreated that night. Sometime during the fight Kennedy was wounded in the left leg. Surgeons were at first optimistic about his recovery, but his condition gradually worsened. He was sent south by train to General Hospital No. 1 at Kittrell's Springs, North Carolina. Admitted on December 9, 1864, Surgeon Holt F. Butt amputated Kennedy's gangrened left leg. Dreadfully weakened from his wound, Kennedy lingered for almost three weeks before dying from "chronic diarrhoea" four days after Christmas.[4]

During the last three weeks of life Kennedy was visited frequently by Reverend M. M. Marshall, the hospital chaplain. In addition to attending to the spiritual needs of the sick and wounded soldiers, Marshall recorded the deaths, burial services, baptisms, and occasional last words of many of the men. William B. Kennedy and 53 other Confederate soldiers who died at the hospital in 1864 and 1865 are buried in a small cemetery in the present town of Kittrell, North Carolina.

Today the community of Kittrell is a quiet crossroads town on State Highway No. 1, 34 miles north of Raleigh. It is still on the rail line that connected it to the war front and the capital city in 1864 and 1865. In the

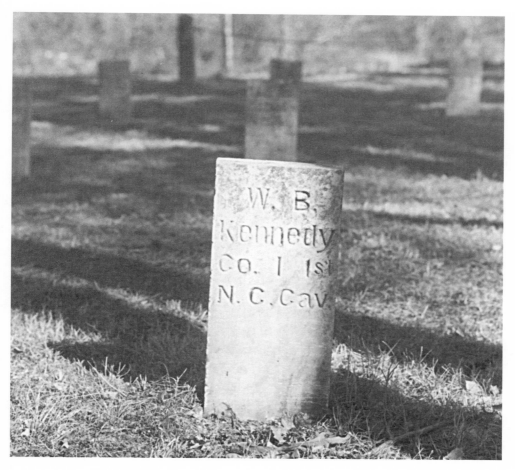

Grave of Private William B. Kennedy in the Confederate cemetery at Kittrell, North Carolina.

1840s a mineral spring was discovered in nearby Long Creek. According to Oscar W. Blacknall, locals enjoyed the cool water with the "curious mineral taste" and

> some who drank it found their health improved. At first a few people in ill health would come and live in tents and drink the water.... In the late forties or early fifties it grew gradually into a rural summer retreat ... [with] some dozens of two room cabins, rude and unplastered.... I was carried there as a very small boy by my father [Charles C. Blacknall]. I recall vividly the long rows

of white washed cabins among the yellow broom straw and the green pines. Dancing was going on under a bush arbor and on a large flat rock up the hill to the northeast of the spring.[5]

In 1858 two brothers from a wealthy family, Dr. George W. Blacknall and Charles C. Blacknall, and their half first-cousin, Thomas H. Blacknall, bought the springs and 200 acres of surrounding land. Construction of four new buildings began immediately. "The place was rapidly transformed," wrote Oscar Blacknall, and "the rude cabins brushed

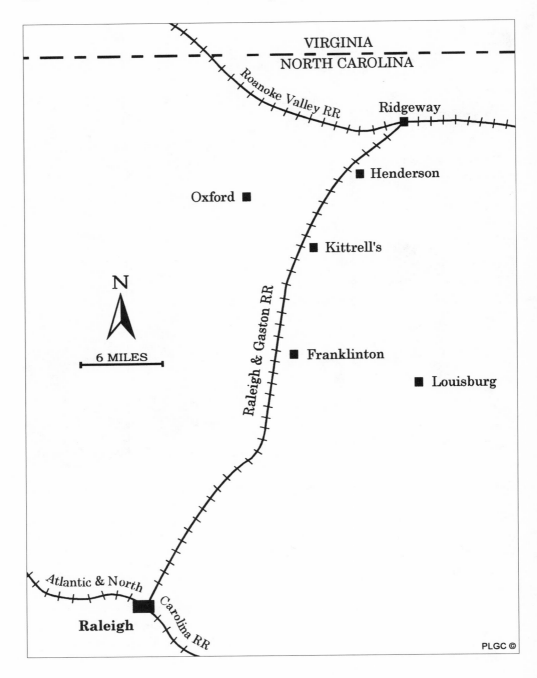

Central North Carolina during the Civil War (author's collection).

aside."[6] An article in the *Raleigh Standard* stated that "from the Springs eastward … rises a hill … [and] about midway on a conspicuous and beautiful eminence, are the hotel domiciles."[7] The main building was 100 feet in length and 60 feet wide, three stories high, with fronting columns two and a half feet in diameter. Inside were 36 large, well-ventilated rooms, a spacious dining hall, and a ballroom. The ballroom floor was "slick as glass, and made of heart pine timbers, two by six inches laid not flat but set up on edge, making the floor half a foot thick." The Long House was two stories high, one room deep, and several hundred feet long. Each level had a porch running the length of the building. Two smaller buildings housed a bowling alley, billiard tables, and a barroom.[8] Oscar Blacknall recalled that

fine turf was found on the stiff lands of the old Burns place. White stones were brought from the rocky ledge half a mile to the south of the springs and broken very small for the walks. Hundreds of shade trees were set out, mostly of elm…. My father's favorite tree was the sycamore and he set a long row of them along the road that then circled the place.[9]

The new regime began in 1860. Families came in their private carriages with their servants, seeking amusement and recreation. From the remote malarial counties to the east they came by rail, seeking health…. With brass instruments by day and string instruments by night, the Springs were kept agog with rollicking merriment. People who lived at home in roomy mansions were willing to crowd four, six, and even eight in a room…. In this way, Kittrell Springs which, as accommodation now goes, would house a hundred and fifty guests,

then often had five hundred. Kittrell Springs, the virtue of its waters, the marvel of their cures, was on every tongue. It was then, and long afterwards, a very beautiful place. The turf was green as emerald, the graveled walks as white as Parion marble.[10]

The year 1861 brought secession. When war became imminent, Charles Blacknall immediately began to organize a company of troops from Granville County. He traveled the county[11] and made speeches in front of town halls and on dusty main streets, urging the young men to defend their homeland. "I may perhaps never have the gratification of reviewing these pages after the conclusion of the war," wrote Charles on the opening page of his journal, "as there is no telling which way the Yankees may shoot in battle, and some stray ball might suddenly make me 'adorn a tale' instead of living to relate to it, but live … or perish I am resolved to do my duty and to use what means I can command towards a vigorous prosecution of this unjust and unholy war, in which we have been forced by our unnatural enemies of the North."[12]

The company that was raised was originally called the Dixie Guards and the name was later changed to the Granville Rifles. "Much of the drilling was done in the grove at the Springs," wrote Oscar Blacknall.

Time without number did the men march and counter-march, double quick, file right, file left, in the beautiful white graveled walks…. Muskets had not yet been issued, so they used tobacco sticks to drill with. Their uniform was black pants and red flannel shirts. These shirts were of such a flaming red that from the

Major Charles C. Blacknall, photographed during a stay in Richmond, Virginia, in November 1862 (*Confederate Veteran*).

hills between the springs and Depot it was easy to desery the men three miles off....

I remember a grand gala ride which the Kittrell wing of the company took to Henderson to join that wing and drill.... We had music and a flag borne in the foremost wagon. There was so much cheering and so much excitement that they forgot to lower the flag as they drove through the grove at Union Chapel, got the flag tangled in the tree limbs and had to stop to disengage it. A great crowd met us in Henderson and there was the inevitable barbecue.[13]

In a letter from camp headquarters in Henderson dated May 27, 1861, Charles noted: "I write this amid a tornado of noise and confusion and have only to say that camp life is more pleasant than you would think. All the little inconveniences of cooking, etc., drinking Champaign out of <u>tin cups</u> and eating half cooked food is not so annoying as you may suppose."[14] Two weeks later, Charles Blacknall, at age 30, enlisted in the Confederate Army on June 11, 1861, as Captain of the Granville Rifles,[15] which later became Company G of the 23rd Regiment of North Carolina Troops. The men from Granville County marched from Henderson on July 6 and arrived in Richmond, Virginia, July 17 to join the Army of the Potomac under the command of General P. G. Beauregard. It was the last time many of them would see home.

Except for the death notices of her young men and the military traffic along the Raleigh and Gaston Railroad, Kittrell's Springs had not physically experienced the war. The fighting in the eastern theater had been to the north. While his two business partners were serving in Confederate regiments, Dr. George W. Blacknall managed the resort. Life at the Springs continued unchanged through the first three years of the war.[16] Business was profitable. The rooms were filled during the summer seasons, the idyllic grounds enjoyed by the strolling, well-dressed guests. Bands played long into the night. Kittrell's Springs was comfortably insulated from the war.

In 1864 the war moved closer to Kittrell's Springs with the Petersburg campaign. With masses of troops just to the north in Virginia and constant skirmishes and attacks along the entrenchments, a steady procession of Confederate casualties moved to the rear along the rail lines. According to local history, a Granville County resident, Mrs. Sarah Elliot, opened her home to the sick and wounded soldiers in the area.[17] Because of the prospect of a long-term struggle at Petersburg, the location of Kittrell's Springs on the railroad, and an already established population of the sick and wounded, the Confederate government impressed the Kittrell's Springs Hotel and converted it to a hospital.

In a letter to his brother George dated May 20, 1864, Charles Blacknall wrote, "I am not surprised or disappointed at the announcement that the Springs has been taken for a hospital.... I hope you will be able to make such arrangements with the Surgn in charge as best to protect the property & make the loss as light as possible. Your idea to secure a position as Steward is a good one, as you will then have charge of the whole business & can protect the rooms, the grounds, &c. The government should pay you $40[000] to 50,000 rent, but that may be too high an estimate, so you can make the best terms possible under the circumstances."[18]

The opening of General Hospital No. 1 was first announced in the *Raleigh Daily Confederate*[19] on June 18, 1864:

Surgeon Holt F. Butt, photographed in 1859 while a member of the Virginia Militia (courtesy Marshall W. Butt, Jr.).

Kittrell's Springs, N.C.

This popular place of summer resort is now open for the reception of our sick and wounded soldiers—as we have turned it over to the government for their benefit. All communications must be addressed to Dr. BUTT, Surgeon in charge.

Blacknall & Co.,
Proprietors

An anonymous letter[20] in the June 28, 1864, edition of the paper states "The place is now under the supervision of Dr. Butt, Surgeon in charge, with Drs. Drake and Berry as assistants, and Dr. Blacknall as Steward and general superintendent. About 300 men have already arrived, and every train brings in a new lot; and as the hospital has just been established and the men have nothing to go on but Government rations, any contributions whatever will be thankfully received. The articles mostly required are milk, butter, fowls, eggs, fruits, vegetables, pickles, cakes, old linen rags, or, in fact, anything will be acceptable. During the past week ... citizens of Oxford, through Mrs. Elliott contributed a wagon load of delicacies—too numerous and good to mention."

Holt F. Butt was born in Portsmouth, Virginia, in 1835 and received his medical degree from the University of Pennsylvania in 1856. With the outbreak of the war, Dr. Butt was commissioned assistant surgeon and assigned to the 32nd North Carolina Infantry. After treating the wounded on a number of battlefields including Gettysburg and Bristoe Station, Surgeon Butt received orders in November 1863 to command General Hospital No. 5 in Wilmington, North Carolina. Within six months Butt

had left to establish General Hospital No. 1 at Kittrell's Springs.[21, 22, 23]

The first patients were received in the second week of June 1864, when eight soldiers were admitted. By the third week, only 42 of the available 265 beds were empty.[24] The hospital staff consisted of Dr. Holt F. Butt, surgeon in charge, two to three assistant surgeons, a steward, and a number of ward matrons, nurses, cooks, and launderers. The August 10, 1864, edition of the *Raleigh Daily Confederate*[25] published a letter from "A PATIENT":

I having been an inmate of this place, feel under obligations to acknowledge the attention received from the ladies of this and the surrounding communities. This hospital being located in the country cold not be visited ... as often as if it were situated in the city, but this difficulty has been somewhat overcome by the weekly visit of the ladies, who bring with them large quantities of delicacies and place them in the hands of the Steward, who makes a liberal distribution of them among the patients.... We shall be pardoned for venturing a suggestion to those who come here on errands of mercy. I think it is not deemed desirable that large numbers of ladies should visit the wards at the same time. This often produces in very sick patients unusual excitement which often results in injury....

It has been but a few weeks since this hospital commenced operations; yet under the supervision and control of Dr. H. F. Butt, Surgeon in charge, it has attained a proficiency not surpassed by many of long standing. In the Medical Department, Drs. Jones, Drake, and Berry, who have their respective wards, are untiring in their efforts to alleviate the suffering and by kind words or sallies of good humor often revive the spirits of the desponding. In the culinary department, Dr. G. W. Blacknall has exhibited his usual ingenuity in supplying every edible that the markets afford which is palatable or nutritional for the sick. Indeed, considering the hardness of the times, and the scarcity of provisions, it is marvelous what a variety of dishes, and well served up, are daily placed upon the table.

In its general management, Dr. Butt has shown himself fully competent to carry on with success an enterprise which is admitted by all to be encumbered with numerous difficulties. His position is one which requires the greatest decision of character, a deep insight into human nature, and an exercise of the most patient forebearance; yet his long service in the field, his experience in the hospital at Wilmington, together with his native ability, qualifies him for the responsible position he now occupies. The friends of the suffering may congratulate themselves on having such an asylum for those who have been wounded or worn out in their country's service.

* * * * *

A resident of Yorkville, South Carolina, Private C. Watson joined the Confederate Army in February of 1863 and served with the 27th South Carolina Infantry. He was sick most of the fall and early winter of 1863, and returned to duty at Fort Sumter in January 1864. Watson was stricken by dysentery in June and was hospitalized at Jackson Hospital in Richmond. He later returned to Jackson Hospital in October, suffering from rheumatism. Watson was discharged for a short time before being re-admitted in December with dysentery. In February 1865 he was in General Hospital Number Eight in Greensboro, North Carolina, bedridden with rubella (measles). Private Watson

was transferred to Kittrell Springs on March 13, 1865, where he died suddenly ten days later from chronic diarrhea.

* * * * *

In addition to the medical staff at General Hospital No. 1, the soldiers there depended on Reverend Matthias Murray Marshall, the hospital chaplain. Marshall was born in Chatham County, North Carolina, and began his studies at Trinity College in Hartford, Connecticut. With the outbreak of war in 1861, Marshall returned to North Carolina to complete his education and was ordained an Episcopal priest in 1863. In December of 1863 he was appointed chaplain to the 7th Regiment of North Carolina Troops; however, he was "taken sick from exposure and left the regiment shortly thereafter."[26, 27]

In March 1864 Marshall became the minister at St. James Parish near Kittrell's Springs.[28] Every Sunday morning Reverend Marshall walked three miles to the parish to deliver his services. On these mornings he would stop and share breakfast with the George W. Blacknall family.[29] On Sunday evenings Marshall preached to a congregation of slaves at a private residence in the area.[30] In June Marshall became the chaplain of the newly established General Hospital No. 1.[31]

The chaplain was never far from the men at the hospital. He visited the wards regularly and moved among the rows of bedridden soldiers, conversing and praying with them. He comforted the dying and prepared them for death, and was perhaps the only attendent at some of their bedsides in their last hours. Marshall consoled the relatives

Reverend Matthias Murray Marshall, probably early postwar (courtesy North Carolina Division of Archives and History).

and families who chose to journey to the hospital, often over long distances, to be with a loved one. Some soldiers near death desired to be baptized. Reverend Marshall delivered the graveside services for those who died and conducted Sunday services with the soldiers. But perhaps most importantly, Marshall recorded the names and regiments, the causes of death, baptisms, last words, and personal observations for most of the soldiers buried in the hospital cemetery. If not for these brief glimpses into the lives and personalities of these men, and the hardships they suffered, they would merely be faded names on gray headstones, their individuality lost to history.

Over 2,106 soldiers were treated at General Hospital No. 1 from June 1864 to April 1865. This figure was totaled from the weekly and monthly "consolidated reports of the sick and wounded" for the hospital.[32] Seven deaths recorded by Reverend Marshall in April 1865 indicate the hospital operated during the first three weeks of that month. With the repeated defeats of the Confederate forces in southern Virginia and North Carolina in the spring of 1865, the number of soldiers admitted to the hospital in April was likely to be high (possibly 400 to 450 men).

It has been estimated that of the approximately 623,000 Union and Confederate soldiers who died in the war, 388,580 (62 percent) perished from disease—chiefly typhoid fever, diarrhea and dysentery, respiratory illnesses such as pneumonia and tuberculosis, measles, and smallpox.[33, 34] At General Hospital No. 1, only 17 percent of the patients suffered from war wounds; the rest were ravaged by the various diseases which plagued the Confederate soldier. Of these, nearly a quarter (20 percent) were stricken with the "blood fevers" and "fevers of the nervous system," the most feared being typhoid fever. Another blood fever, rubella (measles), afflicted 16 percent of the sick patients. Chronic and acute diarrhea, probably the most hated and one of the most debilitating conditions, was suffered by 13 percent of the men. Three percent of the soldiers were hospitalized with "diseases of the thorax," most notably pneumonia and catarrhus simplex.[35]

* * * * *

James Taylor McDow was born September 16, 1829, in Fort Mills, South Carolina, the seventh of ten children raised by Taylor and Nancy McDow. His grandfather, Thomas McDow, served with General Francis Marion during the Revolutionary War. J. T. McDow enlisted as a private in Company H of the 4th South Carolina Cavalry in March 1862, and was later promoted to the rank of sergeant. Suffering from acute hepatitis, McDow was admitted to General Hospital No. 1 on January 26, 1865. As his condition deteriorated, he admitted to Reverend Marshall that he was prepared for death. After he died on February 15, he was buried in the small Confederate cemetery near the hospital.

J. T. McDow and his wife Mellisa were the parents of two children, the youngest of which, Mary Francis, was born after he left for the war. His family never heard from him again, and thus he did not know of his daughter's birth.

He did not return at the end of the war and for 36 years no member of his family could learn of his fate. A fellow soldier noticed his name in the *Confederate Veteran*, and his family finally learned that James Taylor died from acute hepatitis on February 15, 1865, at General Hospital No. 1. It is likely he never fully recovered from chronic diarrhea, for which he was hospitalized in Richmond during August and September 1864, and that may have weakened him in the harsh winter months that followed, during which time he contracted hepatitis.

* * * * *

According to slightly conflicting records, 66 or 68 soldiers died at General Hospital No. 1.[36] From the known causes of death for 54 of these men, the leading killer was typhoid fever (28 percent), followed by pneumonia (20 percent), chronic diarrhea (9 percent), rubella (7 percent), and "vulnus sclopeticum," or gunshot wounds (7 percent). Among these, the deadliest were pneumonia and typhoid fever: 31 percent of all typhoid patients and 36 percent of all pneumonia patients died. Less than five percent of the soldiers who suffered from other diseases or wounds died from their afflictions.[37]

As in the cases of Private Watson and Sergeant McDow, these illnesses were often interrelated. A soldier recovering from one illness typically was so weakened that he was soon attacked by others, either in the hospital or after returning to duty. One of the hardest and most demoralizing battles the Confederate soldier had to fight was that of disease, which poor rations and unsanitary camp and field conditions made nearly impossibly to avoid. Sickness swept through the winter camps and the summer trenches, killing even the toughest and most seasoned soldiers.

* * * * *

The summer of 1864 found the 56th Regiment of North Carolina Troops defending Petersburg. "Our first duty now is making our ditches," wrote one member of the 56th, "that we will in all probability, occupy for some time.... Brush is brought in from the rear to construct booths for shade, and blanket houses are set up and staked by a simple device with horizontal poles or forked sticks.... We are becoming familiar with a new engine of destruction, the mortar gun ... for days the losses on both sides are considerable from this annoyance.... Sharpshooting and mortar-shelling go on briskly ... occasionally a man is struck through the little port hole made for his rifle.... Now for days we have incessant rains; great sickness follows, and disease from the exposure is claiming more victims than the missiles of death."[38]

W. Sutton, a teenaged private in the 56th North Carolina Infantry, contracted typhoid fever in the trenches. Greatly weakened, he was delivered by train to General Hospital No. 1 to recover. Delirious and bedridden, Sutton died on August 2, 1864.

* * * * *

Measles and diarrhea were the two diseases that cut down the most fighting men. Although relatively few soldiers died from measles alone, it was one of the most feared because of its "sequelae," or after-effects. "It is the

peculiar characteristic of measles," concluded a report by the Confederate Pro-
visional Congress dated January 29,
1862, "that the system is left liable to the
invasion of the most formidable diseases,
upon exposure a short time after under-
going an attack. Fever, pneumonia, and
diarrhoea ... followed in the wake of
measles where the convalescents are
exposed to the cold and wet; and when
to this we add unsuitable diet, badly-
ventilated tents and hospitals, there can
be no surprise at the number of sick in
the Army, as well as the great suffering
and distress."[39] From this point of view,
a Confederate surgeon maintained that
"the disease consequent to and traceable
to measles cost the Confederate Army
the lives of more men and a greater
amount of invalidism than all other
causes combined."[40]

Although a symptom of many illnesses rather than a disease itself, acute
and chronic diarrhea were almost un-
avoidable to the Confederate soldier. It
has been estimated that nearly nine-
tenths of all Confederate recruits were
attacked by diarrhea and dysentery at
some time during the war, and were so
weakened physically that they became
easy victims for other diseases. Diarrhea
was probably the most demoralizing
illnesses that could be contracted, particularly in its long-term complications. "The disease that seemed to break
down the will power more than any
other," wrote a Southern minister,[41] "was
chronic diarrhea, and the patients
seemed to lose not only desire to live but
all manliness and self respect." According to one Confederate surgeon "chronic
diarrhoea was very prevalent and quite
difficult of management.... The camp-

ing grounds, privies everywhere, and too
often the depots, streets, etc., of villages
and town presented disgusting evidence
of this fact."[42]

"These disorders [diarrhea and
dysentery] occurred with more fre-
quency and produced more sickness and
mortality than any other form of disease," stated the *Medical and Surgical
History of the War of the Rebellion*.[43]

They made their appearance at the very
beginning of the war.... Soon no army
could move without leaving behind it a
host of the victims. They crowded the
ambulance trains, the railroad cars, the
steamboats. In the general hospitals they
were often more numerous than the sick
from all other diseases, and rivaled the
wounded in multitude. Finally, for many
months after the cessation of the war,
and after the greater portion of the
troops had returned to their homes,
deaths from chronic diarrhoea and
dysentery contracted in the service continued to be of frequent occurrence
among them.

Confederate surgeon Joseph Jones
wrote: "Chronic diarrhoea and dysentery were the most abundant and most
difficult to cure amongst army diseases
... and progressively increased, and not
only destroyed more soldiers than gun-
shot wounds, but more soldiers were
permanently disabled and lost to the
service from these diseases than from
the disability following the accidents of
battle."[44]

*   *   *   *   *

William W. Latham was 38 years
old when he joined the Confederate service in February of 1863 at Pickens,
South Carolina. A farmer of fair com-
plexion and six feet two inches in height,

Latham served with Company K of the 6th South Carolina Cavalry. His health began to deteriorate soon after, being on sick furlough from April to July. Latham was sick or weakened much of the time, as indicated by the following letter written to General P. T. Beauregard by concerned officers:

> We the friends of private W. W. Latham ... do humbly beg that you discharge him from service as he is entirely unfit to perform the duties of a soldier; he is laboring under a severe attack of rheumatism so much so that he has not been able for duty for the last five months.... He has served his country faithfully & has been one of our most worthy soldiers thru the war. Therefore we beg that you discharge or furlow for some 2 or 3 months that his health may be repaired....

This letter was written shortly after he had returned from his first sick furlough. There is no record of any other discharge for W. W. Latham. On August 8, 1864, Latham died of "dyspepsia" at Kittrell's Springs, leaving $18.00 and a silver watch for his wife to claim.

* * * * *

The Junior Reserves

Due to the enormous loss from battlefields and disease, and increasing rates of desertion, the Confederacy was faced with a growing shortage of men toward the end of 1863. For the first three years of the war the North and South participated in periodic, man-for-man prisoner exchanges. These were more important to the South, since the North had a relatively unlimited supply of recruits. The exchanges helped the Confederacy retain its veteran soldiers and replenish its ranks. Understanding this, General U. S. Grant, after taking control of the Union forces in 1864, refused to continue the prisoner exchange system. This decision staggered the Confederacy and doomed many Union prisoners in already overcrowded and underprovided Southern prisons to greater suffering, and often death by starvation and disease.

By the beginning of 1864, nearly all the eligible men in the South (ages 18 to 45) were serving in the Confederate Army. In a desperate effort to secure more soldiers, the Confederate Congress passed an act on February 17, 1864, that changed the age of conscription to 17–50.[45] The young men of age 17 who filed down the dusty roads to the training camps that spring, many of them farm boys leaving their homes and families for the first time, became the North Carolina Junior Reserves. Although rigorously trained, the Reserves were poorly clothed and equipped, often shoeless, and it was all too common that the only shelter that separated them from the cold or wet ground was a blanket. Originally the Reserves were organized only to see duty within North Carolina's borders— once trained and organized into regiments, they were put to work guarding bridges and railroad crossings, and chasing marauders. However, their willingness to do more is illustrated by the following letter:[46]

Camp of Junior Reserves
Near Weldon, N.C. Otober 10, 1864

Hon. Secretary of War, Richmond, Va:

Sir:—We, the undersigned Field Officers of the Junior Reserves of North Carolina stationed near Weldon, N.C., at the unanimous request of the officers and enlisted men of the commands, respectfully tender their services to the department for duty in Virginia during the present emergency, while our National Capital is threatened and its brave defenders stand in need of reinforcements.

The First and Second Junior Reserves (the 70th and 71st Regiments of North Carolina Troops) saw their first action at Belfield, Virginia, when they were hurriedly advanced from their winter camps in North Carolina to meet an advance of Union troops. In a dispatch dated December 7, 1864, General U. S. Grant wrote that "General Warren, with a force of about 22,000 infantry, six batteries, and 4,000 cavalry, started this morning with the view of cutting the Weldon Railroad as far south as Hicksford."[47] On the following day, December 8, the Junior Reserves and regiments of North Carolina cavalry were rushed to Hicksford to defend the railroad bridge that spanned the Meherrin River at Belfield. On December 9 Warren's advance was stopped at Belfield by the fierce resistance of the Confederate defenders. A member of the 5th North Carolina Cavalry wrote "and oh! How those boys [the 70th and 71st Regiments] did fire. They seemed to be taking their 'Christmas' then, in fire works at least. They made their lines lurid in the darkness. And a courier had to be sent down to them 'to stop their

firing'…. It was one of the most terrible nights of cold and rain and sleet our regiment ever saw. The ground and trees next morning were all covered with ice, under whose weight great limbs broke and crashed to the earth…. That morning I saw those same boys following in the pursuit, some of them almost barefooted."[48] A member of the 71st Regiment remembered that "the weather was intensely cold and the boys, poorly clad and badly fed, suffered terribly from exposure, though only a few were killed or wounded in the fight."[49]

The Reserves also played a major role in the battle of Bentonville, North Carolina. From March 19 to March 21, 1865, a force of 21,000 Confederates under the command of General Joseph Johnston battled General Sherman's Left Wing, a force of 30,000 seasoned fighting men advancing toward the capital city of Raleigh. The Reserves were in some of the hottest fighting and forced back several charges against their lines. General Robert F. Hoke, the commander of the Junior Reserves, wrote,

The question of the courage of the Junior Reserves was well established by themselves in the battle … of Bentonville. At Bentonville they held a very important part of the battlefield in opposition to Sherman's old and tried soldiers and repulsed every charge that was made upon them with very meager and rapidly thrown up breastworks. Their conduct in camp, on the march, and on the battlefield was everything that could be expected from them, and, I am free to say, was equal to that of the old soldiers who had passed though four years of war. On the retreat through Raleigh, scarcely one of them left their ranks to bid farewell to their friends,

Private J. W. West of the 10th North Carolina Heavy Artillery, sick with pneumonia, was delirious during the last week of his life. Private R. H. Robinson of the 2nd North Carolina Junior Reserves, suffering from pneumonia, prayed frequently with Reverend Marshall, and seemed prepared for death (photograph by the author).

though they knew not where they were going and what danger they would encounter....[50]

Sixteen of the 54 soldiers buried in the hospital cemetery at Kittrell's Springs were members of the North Carolina Junior Reserves, most notably the 70th and 71st Regiments. Although they were the newest to the Confederate ranks and saw service only in the last months of the war, the Junior Reserves lost many men to disease. Without adequate food, clothing, and shelter, they were assaulted in their camps by typhoid fever and pneumonia. Groups of the sick were admitted to General Hospital No. 1 in large numbers, arriving in train cars and wagons. These sixteen young men, ages 16 to 18, all perished from disease, something their youthful strength and courage could not overcome.

The year 1865 brought the end of the war, and most likely the highest flow of casualties to General Hospital No. 1. General Sherman was methodically advancing from the south and defeated Confederate forces at Averasboro and Bentonville, North Carolina, in March of 1865. Successive Union victories in Virginia against crumbling Confederate resistance at Petersburg, Five Forks, Namozine Church, and other running fights in April compelled General Robert E. Lee to surrender his army at Appomatox Courthouse. Three hundred and forty-seven soldiers were received at General Hospital No. 1 in March, the single highest total for one month.[51] No figures exist for the final chaotic month of April, but seven burials recorded by Reverend Marshall that month indicate the hospital operated at least one week beyond Lee's surrender on April 9. Private Lindsey L. Henderson, 3rd N.C. Cavalry, and Private William Anderson Roach, of "Major Hane's Light Dutymen," died there on April 15, 1865, and were the last soldiers to be buried in the hospital cemetery. Chief Surgeon Holt F. Butt and his staff reported to General Joseph Johnston and were among those who surrendered to General Sherman on April 26, 1865.

The trains finally stopped bringing the carloads of the sick and wounded to Kittrell's Springs. The hotel must have stood empty and strangely quiet, looking rough and unkempt, no soldiers lounging on the front steps, the once-emerald lawns matted and rutted and crossed by dirt trails. The men and boys from Kittrell's Springs and Granville County began to return, many of them walking home as the spring began to change to summer. The miles were surely filled with thoughts of home and peace, and of the hardships and sacrifices newly past.

Colonel Charles C. Blacknall did not return to his beloved "Springs." On June 2, 1862, he was promoted to major and transferred to the Field and Staff of the 23rd Regiment of North Carolina Troops following his valorous conduct at the Battle of Seven Pines on May 31, 1862. During the battle he received five flesh wounds and was injured when his horse was killed and fell on top of him. Major Blacknall was captured at Chancellorsville and was later exchanged. During the Battle of Gettysburg he was seriously wounded in the mouth and neck, captured, and confined in the Union prison on Johnson's Island in Lake Erie during the winter of 1863. Following his exchange in March 1864,[52] he was wounded in the ankle while directing his troops during the Battle of Winchester on September 19, 1864. Fearing the immediate retreat would worsen his condition, and conceding to his demands to save his foot, the Confederate surgeons left him to be taken captive by the pursuing Federals. As his condition gradually worsened, the lower third of his right leg was amputated on November 7. "His health gave way under the severe and excruciating pain of his wound"[53] and he died from "exhaustion" on November 13, 1864.[54]

Following the surrender of General Joseph Johnston, Dr. Holt F. Butt was paroled May 9, 1865, and returned to Portsmouth, Virginia, to resume his medical practice. In the first years after the war he was paid for his services in farm produce, bringing it home by horse and buggy. He and his wife Emily were the parents of nine children. In the last years of his life Dr. Butt suffered greatly from arthritis, and needed to be lifted

Postwar photograph of Dr. Holt F. Butt (courtesy Marshall W. Butt, Jr.).

in and out of his carriage by his driver. Holt F. Butt died October 9, 1900, at the age of 65.[55]

Reverend Matthias Murray Marshall married Margaret Susan Wingfield in 1866 and became the Rector of the Emmanual Church in Warrenton, North Carolina. From 1874 to 1907 Reverend Marshall served as the Rector of the Episcopal Christ Church in Raleigh. Maude Murray Marshall, their daughter, married James William Sumner Butt, the son of Holt F. Butt and his wife Emily. Reverend Marshall died October 22, 1912.[56, 57]

In 1865 the Kittrell's Springs Hotel was sold to Reverend Cornelius B. Riddick, who operated a female academy there from 1865 to 1870.[58] In 1872, Thomas H. Blacknall reestablished the building as a hotel, attempting to regain lost patronage:

1986 Confederate memorial service, Kittrell, North Carolina (photograph by the author).

This popular summer resort is now open for visitors. Pleasure seekers and invalids may find here a healthy, pleasant, quiet retreat, with all the comforts of a home.... We have a large Ballroom and good Music, with Croquet, Billiards, Ten-Pins, Shooting Gallery, and Bathing. The Hotel buildings are half a mile from the Depot, in a beautiful shady grove, near the Springs.... The waters permanently cure Scrofula, Dyspepsia, General Debility, and diseases peculiar to Females, as any learned Physician in the State can testify....[59]

Blacknall abandoned the enterprise a short time later, and the hotel burned to the ground in 1885.[60]

On July 6, 1918, Oscar W. Blacknall killed himself after taking the lives of wife and daughter in their home in Kittrell. The *Henderson Daily Dispatch* wrote that

at the time of his death Mr. Blacknall was nearly sixty-six years of age.... His father's death in battle for the Confederacy, when the son was about ten years old, colored and influenced his whole life....

The work of his life was clerking in a store, then farming, then manufacturing tobacco, until about thirty years ago [1888], when he became interested in the cultivation of strawberries, afterwards enlarged into a general nursery, in which he continued with great success. He married early; suffered a nervous breakdown at 36. He was never well physically and sought health in many ways and many lands.... The death of his first-born son, Oscar, early in a most

Postwar photograph of Reverend Matthias Murray Marshall of the Episcopal Christ Church, Raleigh, North Carolina (courtesy North Carolina Division of Archives and History).

promising career; the death several years later of another son; the afflictions during the present spring of a third son; the protracted illness of a married daughter; the distressing condition of the world at war with the apprehension that his only other son and support might be called to the army; all of this in his enfeebled physical condition and advancing years, made a greater burden than he could bear....[61]

The Confederate cemetery at Kittrell is owned and maintained by the Vance County Chapter of the United Daughters of the Confederacy. Each year, on the third Sunday in May, the Chapter conducts a memorial service honoring the 54 soldiers who died in the Kittrell's Springs Hotel and are buried in the cemetery. Four of the men are simply listed as "unknown," and were apparently too exhausted and near death when they were admitted to utter their names or regiments. The hospital is gone, as are the crowds of soldiers, the wagons, the train cars filled with the sick and wounded, the fitful moans of the delirious—the only evidence of the conflict and hardships of a time long past are the four rows of marble markers beneath the tall cedars in Kittrell, North Carolina.

Notes and References

I. The South's "Sunset Charge": The Battle of Dinwiddie Courthouse, Virginia

1. Clark, Walter, ed. *Histories of the Several Regiments and Battalions from North Carolina in the Great War, 1861–1865.* Volume 5. Goldsboro, NC: Nash Brothers, 1901, p. 638.

2. Colston, Frederick M. "Recollections of the Last Months in the Army of Northern Virginia." Southern Historical Society Papers, Volume 8 (1910), pp. 1–15.

3. Grant, Ulysses S. *The Personal Memoirs of Ulysses S. Grant.* NY: Charles L. Webster, 1885, pp. 437–438.

4. Boatner, Mark M. III. *The Civil War Dictionary.* NY: McKay, 1959.

5. Rockwell, A. D. *Rambling Recollections: An Autobiography.* NY: Hoebner, 1920.

6. Harding, Hiram W. The diary of this 9th Virginia Cavalry trooper is in the Museum of the Confederacy, Richmond, Virginia.

7. Gracey, S. L. *Annals of the 6th Pennsylvania Cavalry.* Philadelphia: E. H. Butler, 1868, p. 327.

8. Newhall. "With Sheridan in Lee's Last Campaign." *The Maine Bugle*, October 1894, pp. 297–317.

9. Aston, Howard. *The History and Roster of the 4th and 5th Independent Battalions and 13th Regiment of Ohio Cavalry Volunteers.* Columbus, OH: Heer, 1902.

10. *Personal Memoirs of P. H. Sheridan.* NY: Charles L. Webster, 1888, Volume 2, p. 139.

11. Headley, P. C. *The Life and Campaigns of Lieutenant-General U.S. Grant.* New York: Derby and Miller, 1866, p. 711.

12. Rosser, Thomas L. *Philadelphia Weekly Times*, Volume 8, Number 7. April 5, 1884.

13. Myers, Art. F. The diary of this soldier is in the possession of Mr. John Devine, Leesburg, Virginia.

14. Gordon, Armistead C. *The Memories and Memorials of William Gordon*

157

McCabe. Richmond: Old Dominion Press, 1925, Volume 1, pp. 163–164.

15. Wise, George. *History of the 17th Virginia Infantry, CSA.* Baltimore: Kelly, Piet, and Company, 1870.

16. Paul, E. A. *The New York Times,* April 3, 1865, p. 1.

17. Rockwell.

18. Harris, Moses. "With the Reserve Brigade: From Winchester to Appomatox." *Journal of the U.S. Cavalry Association,* Volume 4, Number 12, 1891.

19. Gracey.

20. Newhall.

21. Porter, Horace. *Campaigning with Grant.* (Reprint). Secaucus, NJ: Blue and Grey Press, 1985, pp. 428–429.

22. Sheridan, Volume 2, pp. 145–146.

23. Humphreys, A.A. *The Virginia Campaigns of '64 and '65.* New York: Scribners and Sons, 1883.

24. Hannaford, Roger. *The National Tribune,* Washington, D.C. September 9, 1886, p. 3.

25. Hannaford, Roger. *Dinwiddie Court House and Five Forks: Reminiscences of Roger Hannaford, Second Ohio Volunteer Cavalry.* Edited by Stephen Z. Starr. *Virginia Magazine of History and Biography,* Volume 87, October 1979, pp. 417–438.

26. Gause, Isaac. *Four Years with Five Armies.* NY: Neale, 1908.

27. Hannaford.

28. Harris.

29. Isham, Asa B. *An Historical Sketch of the 7th Michigan Volunteer Cavalry.* NY: Town Topics, 1893.

30. Gracey.

31. Humphreys, Charles A. *Field, Camp, Hospital and Prison.* Freeport, NY: Books for Libraries Press, pp. 232– 243.

32. Chambers, Henry A. *Diary of Captain Henry A. Chambers.* Edited by T. H. Pearce. Wendell, NC: Broadfoot Books, 1983, pp. 255–256.

33. Gordon.

34. Wise.

35. Gracey.

36. Newhall.

37. Saunderson, L. T .B. This diary is in the possession of the Virginia Historical Society, Richmond, Virginia.

38. *The War of the Rebellion: A Compilation of the Official Records of the Union and Confederate Armies.* Washington, D.C.: U.S. Government Printing Office, 1864–1927. Series 1, Volume 46, Part 1, p. 1299.

39. Foard, Fred. Memoir of Fred Foard. North Carolina Division of Archives and History, Raleigh, North Carolina, pp. 14–19.

40. Tobie, Edward P. *History of the First Maine Cavalry, 1861–1865.* Boston: Emery and Hughes, 1887, p. 391.

41. Clark, Volume 1, p. 439.

42. *Ibid,* p. 439.

43. Clark, Volume 5, p. 639.

44. *Ibid.*

45. Foard.

46. *The Memoirs of Daniel Branson Coltrane.* Raleigh, NC: Edwards and Broughton, 1956.

47. Foard.

48. Franklin, J. Armfield. The diary of this 13th Virginia Cavalry trooper is located in the Douglas S. Freeman Papers, File 173, Manuscript Division, Library of Congress, Washington, D.C.

49. Franklin.

50. Tobie, p. 390.

51. *Ibid.*

52. Franklin.

53. Clark, Volume 5, p. 641.

54. Monie, John Miller. Memoir of John Miller Monie. North Carolina Division of Archives and History, Raleigh, North Carolina, Civil War Collection, Box 71, File 31.

55. Coltrane.

56. Munford, Thomas T. *History of the Battle of Five Forks.* Handwritten manuscript in the possession of Duke University, Durham, North Carolina.

57. Franklin.

58. Newhall.

59. *Official Records*, Series 1, Volume 46, Part 1, p. 1148.

60. Hutter, J. R. "The Eleventh at Five Forks Fight." *Richmond Times-Dispatch*, July 1, 1906, p. 2.

61. *Official Records*, Series 1, Volume 46, Part 1, pp. 1148–1149.

62. Bowen, J. R. *Regimental History of the First New York Dragoons*. Published by the author, 1900, p. 284.

63. Lee, Andrew J. Co. D, 8th Pennsylvania Cavalry. *Grand Army Scout and Soldiers Mail*, November 22, 1884. U.S. Army Military History Institute, Carlisle Barracks, PA.

64. Gracey.

65. Harris.

66. Krick, Robert K. 30th Virginia Infantry. Lynchburg, VA: Howard, pp. 62–65.

67. Lee, A. J.

68. Humphreys, A. A.

69. Clark, Volume 1, p. 472.

70. Franklin.

71. Foard.

72. McFadden, A. *National Tribune*, Washington, D.C. May 19, 1887.

73. Tobie, p. 392.

74. Clark, Volume 1, p. 440.

75. *Ibid.*

76. Lee, A. J.

77. Chambers.

78. Gause.

79. Lang, Theodore F. *Loyal West Virginia from 1861 to 1865*. Baltimore: Deutsch Publishing Company, 1895, p. 169.

80. Hannaford, *Dinwiddie Court House and Five Forks*.

81. McFadden.

82. Barringer, Paul B. *The Natural Bent: The Memoirs of Dr. Paul B. Barringer*. Chapel Hill, NC: University of North Carolina Press, 1949, p. 118.

83. Clark, Volume 5, p. 476.

84. *Ibid.* p. 474.

85. *Ibid.*

86. Barringer, Rufus. "The First North Carolina: A Famous Cavalry Regiment." Booklet on file with the Wisconsin State Historical Society, Madison, Wisconsin.

87. Cardwell, David. "The Battle of Five Forks." Nashville, TN: *Confederate Veteran*, Volume 22 (1914).

88. *National Tribune*, May 19, 1887.

89. *Ibid.*

90. Tobie, p. 393.

91. Rockwell.

92. Tobie, p. 396.

93. Catton, Bruce. *A Stillness at Appomatox*. New York: Doubleday and Company, 1954, pp. 347–348.

94. Hannaford, *Dinwiddie Court House and Five Forks*.

95. Chester, Henry W. *Recollections of the War of the Rebellion*. Wheaton, IL: Wheaton History Center, pp. 149–160.

96. *Ibid.*

97. Humphreys, C. A., p. 241.

98. *Ibid.* p. 239.

99. Cheney, Newel. *History of the Ninth Regiment, New York Volunteer Cavalry*. Poland Center, NY: Martin, Merz and Son, 1901, p. 259.

100. Harris.

101. Hutter.

102. Hebert, Arthur. "War Reminiscences." *Richmond Times-Dispatch*.

103. Coburn, Jefferson. "A Visit to the Battlefield of Dinwiddie Court House." *The Maine Bugle*, January 1895, pp. 53–75.

104. Whitelaw, Reid. *Ohio in the War: Her Statesmen, Her Generals, and Soldiers*. Cincinnati: Moore, Wilstach, and Baldwin, 1868.

105. Huddle, B. J. The diary of this 29th Virginia infantryman is in the possession of Randal Huddle, Rural Retreat, Virginia.

106. Gause.

107. Newhall.

108. Sheridan, Volume 2, p. 153.

109. Paul, E. A. *The New York Times*, April 3, 1865, p. 1.

110. Tobie, pp. 403–406.

111. Reeves, Edward Payson. 3rd Virginia Infantry.

112. Hannaford, *Dinwiddie Court House and Five Forks.*

113. Blackmar, W. W. *Proceedings of Court of Inquiry in the Case of Lieutenant-Colonel G. K. Warren, Corps of Engineers, Late Major-General U.S. Volunteers, Commanding the Fifth Army Corps.* Washington, D.C.: U.S. Government Printing Office, 1880, p. 1021.

114. *Report of the 46th Annual Reunion of the 6th Ohio Veteran Volunteer Cavalry Association.* Warren, Ohio: Ritezel and Company, 1911, pp. 38–42.

115. Gause.

116. Hannaford, *Dinwiddie Court House and Five Forks.*

117. Newhall.

118. Sheridan, Volume 2, p. 156.

119. Chambers.

120. Clark, Volume 2, p. 107.

121. Pickett, La Salle Corbell. *Pickett and His Men.* Philadelphia: 1913, p. 386.

122. Rockwell.

123. Newell.

124. Reese, Francis R. "The Final Push to Appomatox." *Michigan History Magazine,* Volume 28 (3) (1944), pp. 456–464.

125. *Official Records,* Series 1, Volume 46, Part 1, pp. 1263–1264.

126. *Colonial Records of North Carolina, Book I,* p. 466.

127. *Confederate Veteran,* Volume 37, Number 5 (1930), pp. 189–190.

128. Benjamin S. Ewell Papers, Folder 1, Earl Greg Swem Library, College of William and Mary, Williamsburg, Virginia.

129. Foard.

130. *National Tribune,* Washington, D.C. February 21, 1887, p. 8.

131. Woodbury, Augustus. *The Second Rhode Island Infantry, A Narrative of Military Operations.* Providence, RI: Valpey, Angell, and Company, 1875.

132. Howard.

133. Clark, Volume 1, pp. 780–781.

134. *Official Records,* Series 1, Volume 46, Part 1, pp. 1138–1139.

135. Coburn.

136. Chester.

II. "I'll Live Yet to Dance on That Foot!": The Civil War Experiences of Colonel Charles C. Blacknall, 23rd North Carolina Infantry

The principal source for this work is the O. W. Blacknall Collection (P.C. 101) at the North Carolina Division of Archives and History in Raleigh, North Carolina. The collection contains typescripts of Colonel Blacknall's letters and journal entries, and additional material written by his son, Oscar. Organizational information on the 23rd North Carolina Regiment was largely from:

Clark, Walter, ed. *Histories of the Several Regiments and Battalions from North Carolina in the Great War, 1861–1865.* Volume 2. Goldsboro, NC: Nash Brothers, 1901, pp. 180–268.

Jordan, W., and L. Manarin. *North Carolina Troops, 1861–1865: A Roster, Volume 7.* Raleigh, NC: North Carolina Division of Archives and History, 1979.

Wall, Henry C. "The 23rd North Carolina Infantry." *Southern Historical Society Papers 25* (1897): pp. 151–176.

1. Oscar W. Blacknall Papers. P.C. 101. North Carolina Division of Archives and History, Raleigh, North Carolina.

2. Bullock, George. Cited in the Blacknall Papers.

3. Clark, Walter, ed. *Histories of the Several Regiments and Battalions from North Carolina in the Great War, 1861–1865. Volume 2.* Goldsboro, NC: Nash Brothers, 1901, p. 237.

4. Green, Wharton. *Recollections and Reflections.* Raleigh: Edwards and Broughton, 1906, pp. 178–179.

5. Clark, Volume 2, p. 251.

6. Young, John G. "Thin Gray Line of Tarheels." *Confederate Veteran*, Volume 8, pp. 446–447.

III. An Eye for An Eye: An Episode from Missouri's Civil War

1. Asa V. Ladd Papers, on file at the Joint Collection, University of Missouri Western Historical Manuscripts Collection—Columbia and the State Historical Society of Missouri Manuscripts, Columbia, Missouri (hereafter referred to as the Joint Collection, Western Historical Manuscripts, Columbia, Missouri).

2. Compiled Military Service Record, Asa V. Ladd, Military Records Division, National Archives, Washington, D.C.

3. Ladd Family History, courtesy of Mrs. Laverne Papworth, Troy, Michigan, and Mrs. Shirley Ladd, Cape Girardeau, Missouri.

4. *The War of the Rebellion: A Compilation of the Official Records of the Union and Confederate Armies.* Washington, D.C. 1880–1901. Series I, Volume 34, Part 2, p. 485. (Hereafter referred to as the *Official Records*).

5. *Missouri Historical Review*, Volume 80, Number 2, pp. 176–195. State Historical Society of Missouri, Columbia, Missouri, 1986.

6. *Official Records*, Series 1, Volume 13, pp. 166–171.

7. Compiled Military Service Record for Major James S. Wilson, Military Records Division, National Archives, Washington, D.C.

8. Wilson Family History, courtesy of Mrs. Patsy Creech, Troy, Missouri, and Sidney and D. D. Brown, Evanston, Illinois.

9. Compiled Military Service Record for Major James S. Wilson.

10. *Official Records*, Series 1, Volume 48, Part 1, p. 1054.

11. *Official Records*, Series 1, Volume 41, Part 1, pp. 416–417.

12. *Official Records*, Series 1, Volume 41, Part 1, p. 302.

13. *Official Records*, Series 1, Volume 34, p. 213.

14. *Official Records*, Series 1, Volume 22, Part 1, p. 744.

15. *Ibid.* Part 2, p. 678.

16. *Ironton Iron County Register*, October 2, 1913.

17. Compiled Military Service Record, Asa V. Ladd.

18. *Official Records*, Series I, Volume 22, Part 2, p. 174.

19. *Ibid.* Part 1, pp. 286, 300–301.

20. Compiled Military Service Record, Captain Timothy Reves, Military Records Division, National Archives, Washington, D.C.

21. *Ibid.*

22. *Official Records*, Series I, Volume 22, Part 2, pp. 866–867.

23. Compiled Military Service Record, Captain Timothy Reves.

24. *Official Records*, Series I, Volume 22, Part 2, p. 678.

25. *Ibid.* p. 676.

26. *Ibid.* Part 1, p. 743.

27. *Ibid.* p. 766.

28. *Ibid.* p. 784.

29. *Ibid.* Volume 34, p. 506.

30. Interviews with Mrs. Washington Harris (1881, 1889), in the Dr. John Hume Collection, Missouri Historical Society, St. Louis, Missouri. Partial typescripts in the possession of Mr. Jerry Ponder, Mason, Texas.

31. *Official Records*, Series I, Volume 34, Part 4, pp. 652–653.

32. *Ibid.* Volume 41, Part 2, p. 787.

33. *Ibid.* Volume 22, Part 2, p. 643.

34. Statement of Captain Franz Dinger, in the James Wilson Papers, Collection 1994, Joint Collection, Western Historical Manuscripts, Columbia, Missouri.

35. *Official Records*, Series 2, Volume 7, p. 1061.

36. Statements of Michael Zwickey and James Madison Kitchen, in the James Wilson Papers, Collection 1994, Joint Collection, Western Historical Manuscripts, Columbia, Missouri.

37. Statement of James Madison Kitchen, in the James Wilson Papers, Collection 1994, Joint Collection, Western Historical Manuscripts, Columbia, Missouri.

38. General Order 51 by Brigadier General Thomas Ewing, in James Wilson Family History clippings, courtesy Sidney and D. D. Brown, Evanston, Illinois.

39. *Official Records*, Series II, Volume 7, p. 1061.

40. *Ibid.* Series I, Volume 41, Part 1, pp. 307, 424.

41. *Ibid.* p. 722.

42. *Ibid.* p. 627.

43. *Ibid.* pp. 454–455.

44. Letter from William Nevin to Cyrus Peterson, in the Ewing Papers, Library of Congress, Washington, D.C.

45. Interviews with Mrs. Washington Harris (1881, 1889).

46. *Official Records*, Series I, Volume 41, Part 1, p. 644.

47. *Ibid.* p. 652.

48. *Ibid.* p. 652.

49. *Ibid.* p. 644.

50. *Ibid.* p. 644.

51. *Ibid.* p. 629.

52. Compiled Military Service Record, Asa V. Ladd.

53. Ladd Family History.

54. Compiled Military Service Record, John N. Ferguson, Military Records Division, National Archives, Washington, D.C.

55. Compiled Military Service Record, Harvey H. Blackburn, Military Records Division, National Archives, Washington, D.C.

56. *Official Records*, Series II, Volume 7, p. 1062.

57. *St. Louis Democrat*, Monday, October 31, 1864. On file at the State Historical Society of Missouri, Columbia, Missouri.

58. Asa V. Ladd Papers.

59. Suderow, B. A. *Thunder in the Arcadia Valley, Price's Defeat, September 27, 1864.* Southeastern Missouri State University, Cape Girardeau, Missouri, 1986, pp. 66–72.

60. *St. Louis Democrat*, September 30, 1864, p. 1. State Historical Society of Missouri, Columbia, Missouri.

61. *St. Louis Democrat*, September 30, 1864, p. 1. State Historical Society of Missouri, Columbia, Missouri.

62. Suderow, pp. 81–83.

63. *Ibid.* pp. 88–102.

64. *St. Louis Democrat*, Monday, October 31, 1864. State Historical Society of Missouri, Columbia, Missouri.

65. Account of Birdie Hale Cole, *Confederate Veteran*. Volume 22, p. 417.

66. *Confederate Veteran*, Volume 11, Number 8, p. 359.

67. Suderow, pp. 64–65, 110.

68. Statement of Capt. Franz Dinger.

69. *Ibid.*

70. *Official Records*, Series I, Volume 41, Part 1, p. 693.

71. Suderow, p. 112.

72. Peterson, Cyrus, A. *Narrative of the Capture and Murder of Major James Wilson.* A. R. Fleming Printing Company, St. Louis, Missouri, 1906, pp. 10–11. Read before the Pike County Historical Society, January 26, 1906. (Hereafter referred to as the *Narrative of the Capture and Murder of Major James Wilson*).

73. *St. Louis Democrat*, October 31, 1864. State Historical Society of Missouri, Columbia, Missouri.

74. Statement of Capt. Franz Dinger.

75. *Ibid.*

76. Peterson, pp. 12–13.

77. *Ibid.* pp. 12–13.

78. Statement of Capt. Franz Dinger.

79. *Ibid.*

80. *Ibid.*

81. Shira, Francis. "Major Wolf and Abraham Lincoln, An Episode of the Civil War" in *Arkansas Historical Quarterly*, Volume 2, No. 1–4, March–December, 1943. Published by the Arkansas Historical Association, Fayetteville, Arkansas, 1943, pp. 353–358.

82. *Confederate Veteran*, Volume 18, Number 8, pp. 380–381.

83. *Official Records.* Series II, Volume 7, p. 1111.

84. *Ibid.*

85. *Arkansas Historical Quarterly*, Volume 2, Numbers 1–4, 1943, pp. 353–358.

86. *The Collected Works of Abraham Lincoln*, Volume 8, p. 102.

87. *Ibid.* p. 102.

88. *Official Records*, Series II, Volume 7, p. 1118.

89. *The Collected Works of Abraham Lincoln*, Volume 8, p. 116.

90. Asa V. Ladd Papers.

91. Stanton, Donald, J., Goodwin F. Berquist, and Paul C. Bowers, eds. *The Civil War Reminiscences of General M. Jeff Thompson.* Morningside Press, Dayton, Ohio, 1988, p. 294.

92. *Official Records*, Series I, Volume 34, Part 2, pp. 5–6.

93. *Ibid.* Volume 22, Part 2, p. 750.

94. *Ibid.* Part 1, p. 784.

95. Hume, Dr. John. *The Ripley County Massacre.* March 1907, on file at the Doniphan Public Library, Doniphan, Missouri. Possibly part of the John Hume Collection, Missouri Historical Society, St. Louis, Missouri.

96. Interviews with Mrs. Washington Harris (1881, 1889).

97. *Official Records*, Series I, Volume 22, Part 1, p. 784.

98. Hume.

99. Interviews with Mrs. Washington Harris (1881, 1889).

100. Ponder Family Records, courtesy of Mr. Jerry Ponder, Mason, Texas.

101. Hume.

102. *Official Records*, Series I, Volume 22, Part 1, p. 784.

103. Nash, Charles Edward. *Biographical Sketches of Gen. Pat Cleburne and Gen. T. C. Hindman.* Morningside Bookshop, 1977, pp. 170–173.

104. Suderow, pp. 112–116.

105. *Ibid.* pp. 138–142.

106. *Official Records*, Series I, Volume 41, Part 1, pp. 445–452.

107. *Ibid.* pp. 680, 688.

108. *Ibid.* pp. 629, 653.

109. *Confederate Veteran*, Volume 13, p. 226.

110. *Official Records*, Series I, Volume 41, Part 1, p. 631.

111. Edwards, John N. *Shelby and His Men, or The War in the West.* Hudson-Kimberly Publishing Company, Kansas City, Missouri, 1895, pp. 397–398.

112. Courtney, W. J. "The Last Days of the Confederacy," in The Peacock Papers, Collection 1895, Southern Historical Collection, University of North Carolina, Chapel Hill, North Carolina.

113. *Official Records*, Series I, Volume 41, Part 1, p. 313.

114. *Ibid.* p. 314.

115. *Ibid.* pp. 513, 517.

116. *Ibid.* pp. 647–648.

117. *Ibid.* p. 692.

118. *Ibid.* Volume 48, Part 1, p. 475.

119. *Ibid.* pp. 19–20.

120. *Ibid.*

121. *Ibid.* p. 237.

122. *Butler County, Missouri, Volume II.* Butler County Genealogical Society, Poplar Bluff, Missouri, 1988, p. 56.

123. Ladd Family History.

124. *Arkansas Historical Quarterly*, Volume 2, Numbers 1–4, 1943, pp. 353–358.

125. *Confederate Veteran*, Volume 19, p. 240.

126. Compiled Military Service Record, John N. Ferguson.

127. Diocese of Missouri Archives, Episcopal Church, St. Louis, Missouri.

128. *Norfolk News*, Norfolk, Nebraska, Thursday, July 22, 1897, pp. 17, 19.

129. Highlights in the History of Trinity Church, Norfolk, Nebraska, courtesy of Mrs. Marian Barnett, Trinity Church.

130. Boatner, Mark. *The Civil War Dictionary*. David McKay Company, Inc., New York, 1959, p. 737.

131. Wakelyn, John L. and Frank E. Vandiver. *Biographical Dictionary of the Confederacy*. Greenwood Press, Westport, Connecticut, 1977. pp. 355–356.

132. Wilson Family History.

133. Wilson Family History.

134. *Ibid.*

135. *Ibid.*

136. Extract from the diary of Simon U. Branstetter, in the Thomas Ewing Collection, Library of Congress, Washington, D.C.

137. Branstetter Family History, courtesy of Mrs. Edward E. Lawson, Bowling Green, Missouri.

138. Frost, Capt. Griffin. *Camp and Prison Journal*. Quincy, Illinois, 1867. Also excerpted in the *Kearny-Kennerly Scrapbook* (1872–1910), Missouri Historical Society, St. Louis, Missouri.

139. *Official Records*, Series I, Volume 13, pp. 719, 909; Volume 22, Part 1, pp. 818–819; Volume 22, Part 2, p. 5.

140. *Arkansas Historical Quarterly*, Volume 2, Numbers 1–4, 1943, pp. 353–358.

141. *Ibid.* pp. 353–358.

142. *Collected Works of Abraham Lincoln*, Volume 8, p. 223.

143. *Arkansas Historical Quarterly*, Volume 2, Numbers 1–4, 1943, pp. 353–358.

144. *Official Records*. Series II, Volume 6, pp. 912–913.

145. *Ibid.* p. 922.

146. *Ibid.* Series I, Volume 41, Part 1, page 352.

IV. Rebel Resort of the Dead: The History of General Hospital Number One, Kittrell's Springs, North Carolina

1. Compiled Service Record, William B. Kennedy, National Archives, Washington, D.C.

2. Clark, Walter, ed. *Histories of the Several Regiments and Battalions from North Carolina in the Great War, 1861–1865. Volume 3*. Goldsboro, NC: Nash Brothers, 1901, p. 630.

3. *The War of the Rebellion: A Compilation of the Official Records of the Union and Confederate Armies*. Washington, D.C.: U.S. Government Printing Office, 1864–1927. Series 1, Volume 87, pp. 949–953.

4. Compiled Service Record, William B. Kennedy.

5. Oscar W. Blacknall Papers. Private Collection 101. North Carolina Division of Archives and History, Raleigh, North Carolina.

6. Blacknall Papers.

7. *Raleigh Standard*, Raleigh, North Carolina, August 1980.

8. Pearce, S.T. *Zeb's Black Baby, Vance County, N.C.: A Short History*. Durham, NC: Seeman Printery, 1955, pp. 351–355.

9. Blacknall Papers.

10. *Ibid.*

11. *Ibid.*

12. *Ibid.*

13. *Ibid.*

14. *Ibid.* Letter from Charles Blacknall dated May 27, 1861.

15. Compiled Service Record, Charles Christopher Blacknall, National Archives, Washington, D.C.

16. Various references were made to

the success of the Kittrell's Springs resort in the 1861–1863 letters of Charles C. Blacknall in the Blacknall Papers.

17. *State*, Volume 21, No. 47, Vance County, N.C., April 24, 1954.

18. Blacknall Papers. Letter from Charles Blacknall dated May 20, 1864.

19. *Raleigh Daily Confederate*, Raleigh, N.C., June 18, 1864.

20. *Ibid.* June 28, 1864.

21. Compiled Service Record, Holt F. Butt, National Archives, Washington, D.C.

22. Butt Family History, contributed by Mr. Marshall Butt, Portsmouth, Virginia.

23. Confederate States of America Roll of Honor, Surgeon Holt F. Butt, Museum of the Confederacy, Richmond, Virginia.

24. *War Department Collection of Confederate Records*, Chapter 6, Volume 280, pages 25–44, National Archives, Washington, D.C.

25. *Raleigh Daily Confederate*, Raleigh, N.C., August 10, 1864.

26. Compiled Service Record, M. M. Marshall, National Archives, Washington, D.C.

27. Papers of Matthias M. Marshall, Southern Historical Collection, University of North Carolina, Chapel Hill, N.C.

28. Materials from St. James Church, Kittrell, N.C. North Carolina Division of Archives and History, Raleigh, NC.

29. Pearce, p. 353.

30. Secretary's Book.

31. *Ibid.*

32. War Department Collection, Volume 280, pp. 25–44, 188–231.

33. Gragg, Rod. *Civil War Quiz and Fact Book*. New York: Harper and Row, 1985.

34. Burwell, Walter Brodie. *United Daughters of the Confederacy Magazine*, October 1985, pp. 28–29.

35. *War Department Collection*, Volume 280, pp. 188–231.

36. *Ibid.* pp. 25–44, 188–231.

37. *Ibid.* pp. 188–231.

38. Clark, Volume 3, pp. 368–375.

39. Cunningham, H. H. *Doctors in Gray: The Confederate Medical Service*. Baton Rouge: Louisiana State University Press, 1958, pp. 189–190.

40. Cunningham, p. 190.

41. *Ibid.* p. 186.

42. *Ibid.* p. 185.

43. *The Medical and Surgical History of the War of the Rebellion (1861–1865)*, Part 2, Volume 1, U.S. Government Printing Office, Washington, D.C. p. 1.

44. Cunningham, pp. 185–186.

45. Clark, Volume 4, p. 9.

46. *Ibid.* p. 14.

47. *Official Records*, Series 1, Volume 87, p. 24.

48. Clark, Volume 3, p. 634.

49. *Ibid.* Volume 4, p. 29.

50. Robert F. Hoke Papers, Private Collection 64.1–64.3. North Carolina Division of Archives and History, Raleigh, N.C.

51. War Department Collection, Volume 280, pp. 188–231.

52. Compiled Service Record, Charles Christopher Blacknall.

53. Blacknall Papers. Letter from John W. Lawson dated November 17, 1864.

54. Compiled Service Record, Charles Christopher Blacknall.

55. Butt Family History.

56. Papers of Matthias M. Marshall.

57. Butt Family History.

58. Pearce, p. 352.

59. Flyer advertising the Kittrell's Springs Hotel. North Carolina Division of Archives and History, Raleigh, N.C.

60. Pearce, p. 352.

61. *Henderson Daily Dispatch*, July 10, 1918, Henderson, N.C.

Appendix:
Confederate Cemetery
Roster at Kittrell

BAGNALL, *Walter G.*

Private, Company K, 13th Virginia Cavalry. Admitted on December 9, 1864, with peritonitis, Bagnall died two days later. Because Reverend Marshall was absent, he was buried without services.

BARNES, *John Cauty*

Private, Company I, 5th South Carolina Cavalry. Born on February 27, 1831, the 33-year-old Barnes had frequent discussions with Reverend Marshall. His wife and sister were at his bedside when he died on August 3, 1864.

BARRINGER, *Paul A.*

Private, Company F, 1st North Carolina Cavalry. About 34 years of age, Barringer came from Cabarrus County, North Carolina, and was part of General Rufus Barringer's cavalry brigade. Reverend Marshall had numerous discussions with Barringer,

and was impressed by his acceptance of his coming death. He died on April 12, 1865, of erysipelas [edema] of the head—three days after the end of the Civil War.

BEAVER, *W. A.*

Private, Company B, 2nd North Carolina Junior Reserves. A baptized member of the Lutheran Church, Beaver joined the Confederate Army from Mill Hill, North Carolina. After being admitted with the measles on December 9, 1864, he was stricken with typhoid fever and died on January 9, 1865.

BROWN, *Hugh W.*

Private, Company A, 26th South Carolina Infantry. A resident of Harny, South Carolina, Brown was admitted with pneumonia in January 1865. After seeming remarkably improved over several days, he surprised his doctors when his condition suddenly grew worse; he died on January 28.

BROWN, William

Private, Company A, 35th Virginia Cavalry. William Brown was raised in Milford, Virginia. Admitted with a broken thigh bone, he sadly told hospital staff that he was bereft of any family. His leg injury prevented him from being baptized as he neared death because he could not be immersed. Brown died on October 18, 1864.

BRYSON, Thomas A.

Private, Company D, 25th North Carolina Infantry. Private Bryson died on September 25, 1864, and was buried without a service in the Confederate cemetery.

CORZINE, J. C.

Private, Company B, 2nd North Carolina Junior Reserves. Corzine was suffering from pneumonia when he was admitted to the hospital on December 9, 1864. A popular soldier, a crowd of his comrades gathered for his burial service on December 19.

DIXON, W. A.

24th North Carolina Infantry.

DONELLA, Fendell C.

Sergeant, Company G, 11th Virginia Infantry. Died September 29, 1864.

EARNHART, J. A.

Private, Company B, First North Carolina Cavalry. Earnhart was admitted with a serious fever on December 9, 1864. A Presbyterian minister, he and Reverend Marshall prayed together on December 11, the day before his death.

EDWARDS, J. T.

Private, Company D, 5th North Carolina Cavalry. Raised in Lincoln County, North Carolina, Edwards left behind a wife and son to join the Confederate Army. He whispered to Reverend Marshall that he was ready for death shortly before he died on October 10, 1864.

ELEY, James

Private, Company D, 68th Regiment of North Carolina Troops. A resident of the village of Pitch Landing, North Carolina, Eley was brought to the hospital on December 11 suffering from pneumonia. He died six days later.

ELLIOTT, E. C.

Private, Company I, 1st North Carolina Cavalry. One of the few gunshot victims among the patients at General Hospital No. 1, Elliott was admitted on January 8, 1865, with a serious wound in his knee. As his condition worsened, he spoke of his family in Cleveland County, North Carolina. Elliott's health quickly deteriorated, and he died on January 12.

GAY, Marmaduke

Private, Company G, Anderson's North Carolina Reserves. Originally from Rocky Mount, North Carolina, Gay died from diptheria on October 10, 1864.

GILSTRAP, L. J.

Private, Company G, 6th South Carolina Cavalry. A husband and father with several small children, Gilstrap had been struck in the side by a bullet, which could not be removed. He arrived at General Hospital No. 1 in early September 1864. Marshall indicated that although he was in great pain, Gilstrap was always cheerful and calm. He died on September 27.

GIVINS, J. H.

Private, Company F, 2nd North Carolina Junior Reserves. Givens left his home in Walkersville, North Carolina, to join the Junior Reserves. He quickly fell ill, and was admitted to the hospital on December 9, 1864, with measles. Givins later contracted pneumonia, which ended his life on December 21.

GORDAN, J. M.

Private, Company F, 2nd North Carolina Junior Reserves. Born in Wolfsville, North Carolina, this teenaged boy was admitted with pneumonia on December 9, 1864. He died December 17, 1864.

GREEN, Larken M.

Private, Company I, 56th North Carolina Infantry. His brother was at his bedside when he died on August 11, 1864, from chronic diarrhea. Private Green left behind a wife and one-month-old baby.

GREGORIE, William D.

Private, Company A, 3rd South Carolina Cavalry. Although he was from White's Stone, North Carolina, Gregorie served in a South Carolina regiment. He was admitted to the hospital on March 13, 1865, suffering from measles. Erysipelus [edema] developed, and he steadily worsened until he died on March 31.

GRIFFIN, Alexis

Private, Company D, 6th North Carolina Junior Reserves. This soldier from Chatham County, North Carolina, was buried in the hospital cemetery on August 6, 1864.

HAMRICK, E. M.

Private, Company D, 2nd North Carolina Junior Reserves. After leaving Stephens, North Carolina, to join the Junior Reserves, Hamrick became sick and was hospitalized on January 26, 1865. He died from apoplexy on February 12.

HARGROVE, Wesley

Private, Company A, 5th North Carolina Junior Reserves. Suffering greatly from both typhoid fever and pneumonia, this soldier died on August 14, 1864.

HEADRICK, Moses L.

Private, Company C, 1st North Carolina Junior Reserves. Raised in Silver Hill, North Carolina, Headrick was sick most of the time he was in the Junior Reserves. He was admitted to the hospital on April 5, 1865, and died three days later from chronic diarrhea.

HENDERSON, Lindsay L.

Private, Company H, 3rd North Carolina Cavalry. When Henderson died April 15, 1865, he left behind his wife and two-year-old child in Jacksonville, North Carolina.

HOWELL, J. I.

Private, Company E, 2nd North Carolina Junior Reserves. Howell left Piny Mills, North Carolina, to join the Reserves. He was admitted on December 9, 1864, with measles and pneumonia, and died five days later.

JONES, T.

Private, Company F, 68th Regiment of North Carolina Troops. Suffering from typhoid fever and chronic diarrhea, Jones was admitted to General Hospital No. 1 on December 11. Reverend Marshall visited Jones frequently at his bedside. Jones gradually worsened and died on Christmas Day.

KENNEDY, William B.

Private, Company I, 1st North Carolina Cavalry. Raised in Hallsville, North Carolina, Kennedy was wounded during the Battle of Boydton Plank Road on October 27, 1864. He was admitted on December 9, and his gangrenous left leg was amputated above the thigh. Marshall visited him often until his death on December 29.

LENAIR, J. L.

Private, Company K, 7th Georgia Cavalry. After seeming to improve, Lenair died suddenly on August 5, a victim of apoplexy.

LATHAM, William W.

Private, Company K, 6th South Carolina Cavalry. Latham had been ill during most of his time as a soldier, and died of an undisclosed illness. He was buried on August 8, 1864.

LOCKLAIR, John

Private, Company G, 23rd South Carolina Infantry. Born in 1837 near Marlboro, South Carolina, Locklair developed a close relationship with Reverend Marshall. Marshall baptized him before his death on August 1, 1864.

McDOW, James Taylor

Sergeant, Company H, 4th South Carolina Cavalry. McDow left his home town of Fort Mills, South Carolina, to join the Confederate Army. Suffering from acute hepatitis, he was admitted to General Hospital No. 1 on January 16, 1865. He died nearly one month later on February 15, leaving behind a wife and children.

MIMMS, Josiah Samuel

Private, Company G, 11th South Carolina Infantry. A 22-year-old soldier from Charleston, Mimms was a baptized Methodist who was buried in the hospital's cemetery on August 1, 1864.

PRIVATT, H. P.

Private, Company C, 3rd North Carolina Junior Reserves. Leaving Lumberton, North Carolina, to join the Reserves, Privatt was admitted to the hospital on April 5, 1865, with typhoid fever. Delirious and bedridden, he died on April 10.

PRUITT, William H.

Private, 1st North Carolina Cavalry.

RIDDICK, M. A.

Private, Company D, 5th North Carolina Cavalry. Admitted to the hospital on March 4, 1865, Riddick died of typhoid fever on March 15. He left a wife and small child in Iredell County, North Carolina.

ROACH, William Anderson

Private, Company B, Major Hane's Light Dutymen. Originally from Sawyersville in Roberson County, North Carolina, this 22-year-old soldier died from an unspecified disease on April 15, 1865.

ROBBINS, J. A.

Private, Company G, 51st North Carolina Infantry. Robbins died on July 22, 1864, the first recorded death at General Hospital No. 1.

ROBERSON, W.

Private, Hart's South Carolina Battery. A resident of Bradford Springs, South Carolina, Roberson died from pneumonia on January 29, 1865.

ROBINSON, R.H.

Private, Company F, 2nd North Carolina Junior Reserves. Originally from Steven's Mills, North Carolina, he was admitted on January 2, 1865, with pneumonia. He lingered for nearly six weeks before dying on February 20, 1865.

ROBINSON, S. B.

Lieutenant, Company F, 2nd North Carolina Junior Reserves. After being born in Mount Pleasant, South Carolina, Robinson lived in North Carolina, where he joined the Junior Reserves in 1864. He was admitted on January 26, 1865, with an undisclosed disease (possibly encephalitis). Robinson was in great pain, delirious, and raving during his last week of life. He died March 2, leaving behind a widowed mother and brother.

SAUNDERS, L. E.

Private, Company C, 2nd North Carolina Junior Reserves. After entering the hospital with measles on December 9, 1864, Saunders died on December 15.

STARK, E. or J.

Private, Company I, 67th North Carolina Infantry. A resident of Greenville, North Carolina, Stark entered the hospital on March 8 suffering from measles. He later developed a heart infection, and died on April 1.

SUTTON, W.

Private, Company I, 56th North Carolina Infantry. About 18 years of age, this young soldier died of typhoid fever on August 2, 1864.

TODD, R. P.

Private, Company D, 68th Regiment of North Carolina Troops. A resident of Pitch Landing, North Carolina, Todd was admitted on December 11, 1864, suffering from peritonitis. He died one week later.

TUTTERO, Thomas J.

Private, Company B, 10th Virginia Cavalry. A farmer from Davis County, North Carolina, Tuttero was in great pain from tetanus before he died on October 2, 1864.

UNKNOWN

UNKNOWN

UNKNOWN

UNKNOWN

WAGNER, J. C.

Private, Company I, 1st North Carolina Junior Reserves. Wagner died from an undisclosed disease on August 26, 1864.

WATSON, C.

Private, Company C, 27th South Carolina Infantry. Watson, a resident of Yorkville, South Carolina, was admitted on March 13, 1865, suffering from chronic diarrhea. He died suddenly on March 23.

WEST, J. M.

Private, Company B, 10th North Carolina Heavy Artillery. Originally from Bay River, North Carolina, West was admitted March 27, 1865, with advanced pneumonia. He was delirious until his death on April 2.

WILLIAMS, Henry

Sergeant, Company F, 2nd North Carolina Cavalry. Williams died September 27, 1864, from an undisclosed illness.

Other Recorded Deaths

ANDERSON, Joseph John

This 18-year-old soldier was the son of Harry and Martha Anderson of Edgecomb County, North Carolina. He was baptized a few hours before he died of pneumonia on February 16, 1865. His remains were taken home by his twin brother.

PIERCE, Richard Ricks

Private, Company F, 43rd North Carolina Infantry. Born in Halifax County to Richard Meury and Sarah Jane Pierce, R. R. Pierce turned 17 on Christmas Day, 1864. Gravely ill in January 1865, he was baptized shortly before he died on January 11. His mother drove his body home in a wagon.

STARKS, John

Private, Company I, 67th North Carolina Infantry. A resident of Greenville, Starks was near death when he was baptized by Reverend Marshall on April 1, 1865; he died a few hours later.

Index

Boldface numbers indicate illustrations.